PHASE IN

PHASE IN

How Changing Your Mindset Can Lead
to Exponential Career Growth

DAVID RICH

PHASE IN

How Changing Your Mindset Can
Lead to Exponential Career Growth

ISBN   978-1-61961-512-0 *Paperback*
        978-1-61961-513-7 *Ebook*

LIONCREST
PUBLISHING

To my mom and dad for their continued support and wise counsel.

To my sister who made edits that only she could make.

*To my extended family whose support and
encouragement made a ton of difference.*

*To the teachers in the public school system who
saw my potential before I knew it existed.*

CONTENTS

FOREWORD

ALTHOUGH I AM an expert in telecommunications and information technology, I'm far from an ordinary technology guy. From a young age, it has been my mindset that has carried me through my career. A primary goal I have in writing this book is to share my story with you in hopes that you might find inspiration, motivation, and valuable lessons that will help you along your path.

Certainly, we all have different paths to walk in this life. Mine, like many of yours, was not always full of sunshine, but I managed to find and prove myself along the way. My hope is that you, too, will find yourself along the way. As you read my stories, I want you to take what you can from the lessons I've learned and apply them to your own life. I suspect that if you phase in to what's being shared in my story, you will see parallels and subsequent actions for your pathway to success.

And just to be clear, the lessons in the pages that follow do not apply strictly to the field of technology. Although this is a book geared toward tech professionals, anyone can find lessons applicable to his or her own desired career path. If you are willing to cultivate the right mindset from these insights, you will find success in whatever career path you pursue.

INTRODUCTION

TECHNOLOGY IS one of the most rapidly changing fields in the world, and its exponential growth presents a series of challenges for today's tech professional. Because so much has changed so quickly during the last two decades, one's skill set can quickly be rendered obsolete.

As a result of the shifting demands, the job market has been extremely challenging for people in recent years. Anyone not up to date on cutting-edge technology is bound to wind up in a difficult position in terms of career growth. Not being up to speed on the current trends within one's particular field could create a career rut or worse, job loss.

Due to these challenges, technology professionals often

find themselves in awkward positions. Change can be difficult and adapting to rapid change is problematic for many people. In fact, it can be a bit scary. Yet, this is the harsh reality with which we must deal. My goal is to give you the strategies necessary to survive in today's job market...and tomorrow's.

Most people drawn to technology are analytical, left-brained thinkers who love problem solving. They tend to enjoy science, mathematics, and engineering. While this natural inclination has definite advantages, that constant left-brained thinking can sometimes be a hindrance.

For example, I used to be quite the poet. I was constantly reading and writing poems, even *thinking* poetically. My imagination was in overdrive, and I loved the creative process. As I progressed as an engineer, however, I began to lose that creative side of myself. The poet in me died a little as I began nourishing the more logical aspect of my being.

This is a cautionary tale to the tech professional. Beware of losing the ability to tap into your creative side. There are myriad ways the right-brain can be beneficial in this field. When you're troubleshooting a particular technical problem, for example, and you've exhausted all of the technical diagnostics and routines but the problem persists, that problem is often neither procedural nor technical—it's physical. If you're able to tap into your creative side, you will find solutions that your more methodical colleagues often miss. In other words, humanize the process.

Humanizing the profession in a few crucial ways will expand your view and subsequently, open up opportunities that otherwise could be missed. To do that requires a focus on increasing our emotional intelligence. Throughout our lives, we interact not only with things but with people and places as well. As the most complex organisms on the planet, our interpersonal interactions display an astonishing array of variety.

In my travels, I've always been fascinated by different cultures. But as foreign as they might be and despite our language barriers, I have always been able to communicate nonverbally using gestures, body postures, facial expressions, and other cues.

Humanizing the tech field requires instinct. It's also important to know which types of behaviors are considered offensive in a given culture. In the United States, we tend to display aggression in our communication with the use of pitch, tone, and energy levels, which is often considered hard charging and productive.

In places where people are less likely to be as direct in their communication, however, that type of aggressive posture will be seen as antagonistic and might well ruin any chances of making a connection. It's critical, therefore, to take the pulse of any particular environment, observe the surroundings, and get a feel for others' communication processes to determine the best method for interacting.

As technology professionals, it is imperative that we focus on mindfulness, which involves being present in the moment. Often, our minds wander to thoughts about what has happened previously or what might happen later, thus reducing the full engagement of the present moment. A good exercise is to always ask yourself in any given situation what's most important, what happened yesterday, what will happen tomorrow, or what is happening right now.

The tech profession is mired in its focus on rapid reaction, as many meetings tend to devolve into showcases to demonstrate the quickest responses to issues rather than thoughtful consideration of those issues. The best ideas often go unspoken, unconsidered, and unused. Training to focus on emotional intelligence, instinct, and mindfulness is essential to humanizing the tech profession.

A gentle reminder that we are human beings is the best

way out of this rut. Emotional intelligence allows us to detect when someone is monopolizing the discussion, allowing the leader or project manager to engage the entire room, unearthing hidden gems from people who might otherwise remain quiet during the more vocal participants' monologues.

Our instincts empower us to tap into the group dynamics of social situations, making clear who the leaders are and allowing us to make meaningful connections with them. Instincts provide guidance as to when to speak and when to sit back and listen. They are a necessary part of interacting with our fellow humans, and tapping into this natural intuition can only help further our professional lives.

When we are mindful, we're able to learn in a way in which others, in a state of anxiety, simply can't. Early in my career, I worked as a circuit repair technician, often performing routine and repetitive tasks that could have bored me to distraction. Instead, however, I focused my attention on each present moment, which allowed me to learn faster and retain more than my distracted peers. As a result, the company created an entire department for me to lead.

Setting a mindset is the first step. Next, you need to set your intentions on a goal. Then, you have to act. Mindset and intention are meaningless without the corresponding action. The beauty of this is that these three steps can be applied to anything you want in life. These efforts go beyond just technology. There is a clear road map to achieving the desired outcomes in your life. It is my intention to share this precise road map with you.

As I said, I don't consider myself to be a typical information technology (IT) or telecom guy. Rather, I consider myself more of a technologist. And while I reside in the realms of IT, information systems, and telecommunications, I never limit myself to one single area, as I yearn to devour knowledge of all things technology. I appreciate the core mechanisms of technology regardless of what that technology might be. Despite the challenges I've faced, my affinity for technology helped me rise quickly throughout my career.

If there's one thing that has set me apart from my colleagues, it's my thirst for knowledge. I have always sought opportunities to increase my learning and understanding. Opportunities that would otherwise have never arisen have, in fact, presented themselves to me as a result of my having first acquired knowledge of a particular subject.

And while the act of learning for the sheer sake of learning might seem counterintuitive in a world dominated by specialization, that has been the secret to my success. So while others wait for an opportunity to pop up before attempting to accrue the necessary knowledge to take advantage of it, I have worked in reverse fashion, seeking the knowledge initially, only to later discover how it will benefit me.

I knew from the time I was a teenager that I would one day be an engineer. My friends laughed at the notion because I was terrible at math.

"An engineer? Seriously? But you're not even good at math!"

I remember their doubt to this day, but that skepticism only propelled me. I knew what I wanted, and I wasn't going to let anyone stop me.

A funny thing happened after I set my mind on becoming an engineer. Once I established my mindset, opportunities that would lead me down the right path presented themselves all around me in an almost magical way. I set forth my intentions and never once allowed anything to get in the way. The mindset was the baseline, and the intent was the kinetic energy that moved me toward my goal.

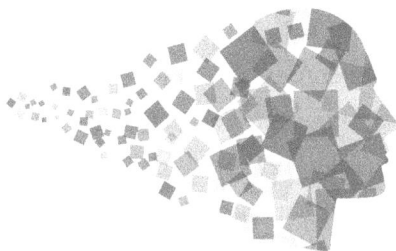

CHAPTER 1

THE PATH IS NOT ALWAYS CLEAR

I GREW UP with modest means in a working-class neighborhood in Baltimore, Maryland. As a teenager, I often struggled with the call of the streets. I loved being out with my friends into the late night hours, just hanging out. Of course, as you may guess, just being out there often put me at risk. I certainly had some close calls as a teenager. I suspect that if you met me when I was sixteen, you'd have a hard time believing that I was going to be an engineer. At that age, I cared only about hanging out and going to parties. In that sense, I was a pretty typical teenage boy growing up in the inner city. Although I appeared to have no real direction at the time, the truth is that behind the scenes, I was building a mindset that would guide my future.

By the time I turned seventeen, I was bored to tears at school. Sit in a fifty-minute class and listen to a teacher drone on and on? No, thank you. I hated it. I started joining clubs on campus just to get out of class. I even joined the glee club (although I had no idea what a glee club was) so that I could get out of class.

When I first enrolled in high school, I chose automobile mechanics as a vocational track. I can't say a lot of thought went into this choice, but it seemed logical at the time. The problem was that from the first day, the shop teacher and I butted heads. We just failed to see eye to eye. I wasn't happy in the class, and it was affecting my desire to complete the assignments.

In fact, one day during class, the shop teacher decided to pick on me for whatever reason. I had seen him do it to other boys in the class and wasn't interested in letting him holler and scream at me like he did to them. At one point, he got right up in my face in the most threatening posture, which made me so angry that I picked up a large iron file and was determined to defend myself with it. Once he saw that I was serious, he backed off and decided to send me to the principal's office.

When I got to the office, the principal, to his credit, decided to hear my side of the story before taking any disciplinary action. It seems that I wasn't the only one complaining about this particular teacher's menacing approach to interacting with his students. So he decided to allow me to transfer into a different shop class, and I chose industrial electronics. Thank God for that principal.

I should note that when I chose industrial electronics as an alternative vocational track, I really didn't give it much thought either. The fact is that I would be starting that track five weeks behind the rest of the class. I have to admit that I was a bit concerned about being so far behind in the class, but it turned out that I quickly got the hang of things and excelled in the coursework. Joining the electronics track was the first step to getting where I needed to be.

Even after this change of course, I was still just gliding through classes. I was the type of student who would do the bare minimum to maintain a C average. I wasn't focused much on school. Then, one day during my senior year, one of the representatives from the National Urban League (NUL) showed up in my homeroom class. He was a young, well-dressed guy who visited the graduating class to talk about the apprenticeship programs that the NUL was working with to place qualified students in various apprenticeship programs.

I was only half listening as he spoke, probably daydreaming about whatever party I'd be going to that weekend, until he said, "If you're interested, I'll be back next Monday, but you'd have to miss your seventh-period class."

Those were the magic words. *You mean that I can get out of seventh period? Oh yeah, sign me up!*

So I signed up for the next lecture on apprenticeships and learned I would have to take a series of aptitude tests, which would take place during class time. For several months, I took one test after another to demonstrate skills in reading comprehension, basic math, logic, geometric evaluations, and so on.

Lo and behold, several days after graduating from high school, I received two apprenticeship offers. One with the Sheet Metal Workers and the other with the International Brotherhood of Electrical Workers unions. I chose the latter with a great deal of excitement. It just felt like the right thing to do.

I arrived for my first day of work on the last day of August, at the peak of the summer heat. Per the instructions I was given, I sought out the foreman, eager to introduce myself and get right to work doing "electrical" stuff.

"Follow me," he said without the slightest hint of a "Welcome aboard" or "Good to meet you." Instead, he gave me a green hard hat and walked me to the back of the building. Actually, it wasn't quite a building yet, just a sixteen-story iron structure without walls.

We entered a fenced-in area about half the size of a basketball court. In the middle of the area was a shack. We walked in.

"Do you see that pipe coming out of the panel going into the ground?"

Of course I saw the pipe.

"Well, somewhere underground," he went on, "that pipe is heading for the building. I want you to find it."

I thought about this for a minute.

"So, you want me to dig a ditch tracing the pipe toward the building?" I asked in disbelief.

After all, the pipe had many routes toward the building, and I couldn't dig inside the shack because it was concrete slab. I would have to dig in the remaining dirt outside.

"That's right," he answered as he handed me a pick, a shovel, and a digging bar before he walked away. Words do not do justice to the scenario in a way that can be truly appreciated. Let's just say, this was a difficult task.

I spent two full days in the hundred-degree heat of a blaring sun, looking for that pipe. Every time I'd put the shovel in the ground, I'd hit rock, which I'd have to break up to make any progress on dirt removal. No matter how far wide or deep down I dug, it seemed the pipe was playing hide-and-seek, never revealing its actual location.

Finally, at the end of the second day, with a sunburned back, weary arms, and badly blistered hands, I found a huge round rock about three-feet deep in the dirt. Something told me to break this rock, so I took the fifty-pound digging bar and kept hitting the rock until at last, it broke in half.

When I pulled up one side of the broken rock, I saw what I had spent two solid days looking for. Directly underneath this rock was the electrical pipe heading toward the larger building structure. Now, this was probably a coincidence, but you should know that those first two days on the job turned out to be a precursor to my entire experience as an electrical apprentice.

For two years, I pushed heavy wheelbarrows of concrete through six inches of mud for a distance of two blocks. I dug deep ditches for electrical piping, carried heavy bundles of flexible steel used to reinforce concrete floors, climbed off the side of fourteen-story buildings and pulled electrical cables through pipes located in mosquito-infested wastewater treatment plants, to name just a few of my greatest hits.

At first, I questioned my decision to become an electrical apprentice. After all, here I was wearing a thirty-pound belt of electrical tools I rarely got to use. And of course, there was the extreme heat—or extreme cold—I found myself working in, day in and day out. There was a point at which I think I started to go a little bit crazy just dealing with the elements.

We were installing electrical equipment in a new auto plant situated right on a waterfront in the dead of winter. All of the exposed steel in the plant made it feel like working in an icebox. I mean, it was seriously cold. On top of that, we were on a critical deadline, so the entire crew had to work ten-hour days for thirty-nine days straight.

By the twentieth day, it seemed everybody was a bit, shall we say, "on edge." The threat of violence lurked tangibly just beneath the surface, waiting for something to spark its appearance. The funny thing was that as the days went on, and it became harder and more uncomfortable, I leaned into it as if I enjoyed every minute of the experience. With the unwavering intention to make it through thirty-nine straight ten-hour days, I came out the other end much stronger and more determined than when I went in. It was an inflection point in my life—one of many to come.

The truth is, the day after my grueling introduction to "electrical work," something inside whispered to me to overcome whatever challenges I encountered. That mindset was the baseline that fed my intentions. And my intentions were clear: Be the best, the strongest, and the fastest apprentice around.

I took the attitude that no matter the obstacle, I would embrace the struggle with fervor, even if that meant standing on the sixteenth floor of a building with no walls, with the wind chill several degrees below zero for weeks at a time. (By the way, I did this for the entire winter of my first year as an apprentice.)

I trained myself to welcome each and every challenge. After this mental shift, I excelled at everything that was asked of me. I'd move at lightning speed to quickly dispatch any task I was assigned.

Unfortunately, my bursts of energy weren't as welcomed as I'd hoped. After a while, it seemed that my foreman might have preferred that I spend a bit less energy. I was moving so quickly that they struggled to keep me busy for the entire day. They'd ask me to dig a ditch, and I'd finish it in record time. My bosses became annoyed with finding me tasks. Nevertheless, I resolved that I would be the hardest worker on the site.

It was during this apprenticeship that I learned to relish problem solving and hard work. I took the jobs that no one else wanted, and I excelled at them. I look back on this period as critical to my mental growth. At the time, I didn't fully understand the impact of this internship. But in retrospect, it was the catalyst for future growth in my career.

Then, suddenly, I was taken off course. The path became unclear again. During the second year of my apprentice-ship, tragedy struck. One of my best friends died. I fell into a deep depression and eventually had to leave the NUL program.

After the apprenticeship program, I worked for a while as a nonunion electrician during the day and as a security guard at night. I decided I wanted to go back to college and get a degree rather than pursue construction work.

I didn't consciously think that this would lead me to my goal, but I just needed to do something more with my life. Getting a degree in electronics just seemed to make sense. I took those classes in high school, so why not? I felt like I needed to have a degree to move on with life, but I had no idea what this decision would ultimately mean for my career and true goal of being an engineer.

Once I got accepted to a degree program at DeVry, I ended up landing a highly coveted internship strictly because of my experience with NUL. Without that apprenticeship, there's no telling whether I would have been selected for that internship. However, because of my experience, I had a slight advantage and was able to get into a competitive internship.

The main lesson I would like to impart from this time in my life is that the path is not always clear. Sometimes you need merely to have intent and take action. Although I had no idea as a sixteen-year-old kid of the journey I was about to undertake, I followed my intuition, which landed me the apprenticeship with NUL, which in turn set the trajectory of my career. When the path is unclear, do not be afraid. Set your intention and move forward along your path. Clarity will come in time.

KEY LESSONS FROM CHAPTER 1

- HAVE THE RIGHT MINDSET.

- SET YOUR INTENTION.

- TAKE ACTION.

- THE PATH MAY NOT BE CLEAR, BUT IT
  WILL BECOME APPARENT IN TIME.

CHAPTER 2

SHARPEN YOUR SKILLS

AS A PROFESSIONAL in any field, you should always be honing your skills. There is never a time where you can sit back and say, "All right, I know everything there is to know." Losing your drive to increase your skill set is a huge mistake. In my life, I've always sought to widen my set of skills, and this has been the key to my success in the field of technology.

When I secured that coveted internship, I was thrilled that all my hard work digging ditches and fetching coffee had finally paid off. I went into the internship with a positive attitude and my work ethic in full force.

On the first day of the internship, one of the technicians brought out a stack of circuit design layout reports, which are diagrams explaining how to wire voice and data circuits. I had never seen circuit design layouts before in my life, so the experience of wiring these circuits was completely new. There were about fifty circuits of various designs within the stack. The technician who was tasked with training me spent about fifteen minutes wiring three or four, then walked away, leaving the rest of the stack with me.

Although he didn't specifically instruct me to continue the task, I decided out of curiosity to see if I could follow through with what he did. I noticed that after he would wire a circuit, he'd then go to a patch panel where it appeared he could test to ensure the circuit functioned correctly.

Because I'd carefully watched him when he tested the circuits, I tried to figure out the test method on my own. I wired a couple, then went to the test board to see if I could find them. After studying the diagram, I realized that the location of the circuits on the patch panel could be correlated to the location of the circuits on the wiring frame.

When I found the two that I had wired on the patch panel, I was dismayed to find they didn't work. When I went back to the wiring frame, I figured out what I had done wrong, corrected it, and went back to test them. This time, they worked.

For the remaining day and a half, I repeated this process almost fifty times until I had virtually all of the circuits wired and tested.

Toward the end of the second day, while I was completing the last of the circuit stack, my supervisor snatched them away from me. He went to the test board and began testing them. I didn't quite understand his negative energy. After all, I had been on the job for less than two days and had very little interaction with him to that point.

In any event, he proceeded to test the first circuit in the stack. It worked. Then he went into the middle of the pile and tested another one. It worked. He went a little further down the pile and tested another one. It also worked. Finally, he went to the end of the stack and tested another one. Again, it worked.

He took off his headphones, put them down on the desk, and walked away. Shortly after that, one of the managing technicians walked up to me and said, "Dave, I probably shouldn't be telling you this, but the supervisor had decided we didn't want an intern. So they were going to let you go. But you did such a good job learning how to wire these circuits in such a short time frame that we want to keep you on and make you a part-time employee instead."

I was a bit shocked that my internship was even in jeopardy, but I was happy that I would get to earn money in addition to learning a technical trade while in college.

The bottom line here was that instead of being fired, I went from being an intern to a part-time employee. The key point was that I came to the position looking for ways to sharpen my skills from day one. If I had been less enthusiastic, I would have been let go on the second day. Had that happened, I have no idea where my career would have gone. Fortunately, I don't have to wonder because I got the opportunity to stay and learn even more. In fact, this is the point where my life in IT and telecom began.

At every inflection point in my career, I decided to go outside my comfort zone and learn a new technology. I never sought knowledge with the thought of being able to use it later. I generally embraced it because I enjoyed the experience of learning something new.

I'm often fascinated by new technical experiences and have on many occasions sought more information about something, whether it was related to my job or not. As I acquired this new knowledge, opportunities started showing up, and my career would advance in that direction.

It is for this reason that I consider myself to be more of an entrepreneur than a typical employee. Entrepreneurs take risks without knowing what the reward will be. Sometimes they fail, but when they succeed, they reap all the benefits of that risk. I've always treated my career more like a business than a job. By having an entrepreneurial mindset and always seeking to sharpen my skills, I've been able to gain direct benefits from my efforts.

The fact is that whatever happened next in my career was almost always directly related to the sharpening of my skills. For example, the company I worked for was building a second network operations center. The technician responsible for building the new center ended up getting into a tiff with the manager and was let go.

The timing of this was pretty bad, as they now had no senior-level technicians available to build the new operations center. Making matters worse, the existing operations center, which was generating the revenue, had to be maintained in the meantime.

So, for whatever reason, they decided to give me the significant task of managing the installation of this very complex network operations center despite the fact that

I was the junior technician in the department at the time. Of course, I jumped at the opportunity. At no point did I feel intimidated by the responsibility. In fact, I welcomed the challenge.

So I set about the task of managing the vendors, working with the designers in developing the floor plans, directing the construction crew activity, implementing the required technical infrastructure, and bringing the site online.

It's important to note here that it was because I took on the task of quickly mastering that initial stack of circuit layout designs and continued to prove my competence in whatever task I was assigned that the company made the unprecedented decision to put the full responsibility of their brand-new network operations facility in my hands. If you're curious, the facility was finished on time, on budget, and fully functional.

Once the new site was operational, I became the lead circuit repair technician. The director decided to create a separate shift for quality control specifically for me. It was my job to run sophisticated diagnostics against all customer-active circuits, confirm the quality of these circuits, and identify for the day crew which ones required additional work to meet the approved standards.

I was in charge of the circuit repair stuff from 4:00 p.m. to midnight. Another person would come in from 11:00 p.m. to 8:00 a.m. and do all of the required computer maintenance as well as billing. He and I made an agreement: I agreed to teach him telephony, and in exchange, he agreed to teach me the computer system. The caveat was that I would work my swing shift and then stick around for his overnight shift. I got paid for only the former, of course.

I worked those double shifts for four or five months while I learned the computer system. Working a second shift without compensation might seem crazy to a lot of people. *Why would anyone work for free?* Well, it was that thirst for knowledge that I just needed to quench. I wasn't satisfied with just clocking in and out; I had to learn more and sharpen my skills. Learning the computer system was not necessary for me to keep my job, yet I felt that I needed to do it somehow. I was hungry for more knowledge and was fortunate to have the chance to learn (essentially free of charge) from my coworker.

The next thing that happened was quite unbelievable. A snowstorm struck one night. By 10:00 p.m., it had dropped three or four feet of snow on the ground. Management called to see if my coworker was able to get in. He wasn't. He had called earlier and said that he couldn't even get out of his driveway. Management was in a panic, concerned that missing the nightly billing would be a nightmare for the company.

"Don't worry about it. If you need me to do it, I'll take care of it," I said.

The district manager was confused, unaware that I had been working double shifts for months figuring out the whole system. After several phone calls and a lot of puzzled voices, they left the nightly billing processing to me, which I took care of.

Early that morning, they rushed in to see what the damage was. To their astonishment, everything was running perfectly; the billing was complete and flawless.

Some weeks after that, one of the supervisors for the computer system decided to leave the company to take a job with a different telecom corporation. I bumped into him on the elevator, and he asked, "Are you happy where you are?"

"Why?" I asked. "You got a job for me?"

"Yeah. Why don't you come and interview?"

So I did. And sure enough, they hired me as a computer systems specialist.

This upward move in my career was the result of all the work that I had put into sharpening my skills and acquiring new knowledge. Without working those double shifts, I would never have had a clue about how to do the billing. The company would have been in an enormous amount of trouble, and I would never have had the chance to show my competency and prove my worth. Because of my ongoing quest for knowledge, I moved into an entirely different department.

Now, you might say that I created my own luck in this situation. However, it's a bit deeper than that. My mindset was right from the beginning. I had decided that I would always be learning and increasing my skill set. Whenever an opportunity arose, I would take it on. Because of my willingness to do what others would not, I was able to take advantage of the opportunities as they were presented.

During this part of my career, I went outside my usual routine and sacrificed comfort to work double shifts. Although there was no rainbow that I could see at the end of that process, I did it anyway just because I wanted to acquire the knowledge.

What I recommend to you, the reader, is to seek a level of mastery in your current station and be constantly on the lookout for opportunities to increase your abilities.

Look out into the marketplace and see what's going to be happening next in your industry. Or take a broad viewpoint of your current job and look for vertical associations to other related disciplines internally. When you find something that interests you, take the initiative to learn as much as you can about it. The more it interests you, the stronger your desire to acquire knowledge about it. The more knowledge you obtain, the better the odds that you'll find a way to benefit from the information.

There were very few people discussing cloud computing fifteen years ago. Now it's a huge topic in technology. The people who jumped on it from the get-go are way ahead of the game. You always want to use your thirst for knowledge as leverage in your chosen field. Don't be the person who just goes to work and does the bare minimum. Always look for opportunities to increase your value not just at your job but also in your neighborhood, city, state, and country.

Take the risk of acquiring new knowledge without worrying about any immediate payoff, and once acquired, be prepared to take action when a new opportunity presents itself. Cultivate and grow your entrepreneurial instincts and treat your career like a business. Use this mindset to be the chief executive of your life.

KEY LESSONS FROM CHAPTER 2

- ALWAYS SHARPEN YOUR SKILLS.

- NEVER QUENCH YOUR THIRST
  FOR KNOWLEDGE.

- KEEP YOUR EYES OPEN FOR
  OPPORTUNITIES TO GROW.

- CULTIVATE AND GROW YOUR
  ENTREPRENEURIAL SPIRIT.

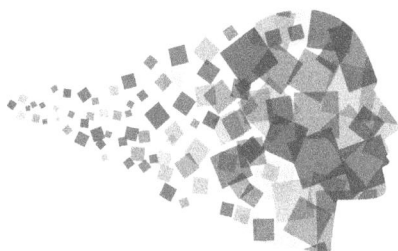

CHAPTER 3

SLAY THE DRAGONS AS THEY COME

ONE KNOWN FACT of life is that there will always be challenges, some more trying than others. It's not uncommon for those challenges to show up at the most inopportune times. Maybe you just got a new position at work when you discover the company is merging with another organization that already has that role covered, essentially making you a redundancy. Maybe your boss puts you up for a promotion but is fired before it's official, thus derailing your advancement. Or maybe the technology you spent years mastering is suddenly decommissioned from the network because the vendor went out of business (true story).

Are you able to identify the opportunity in any of these scenarios? If you can't, you simply need to shift your mindset. Suppose you looked at every challenge or difficulty as an opportunity to increase your skill set, grow experientially, and gain knowledge and wisdom. What if you welcomed change and embraced the resultant struggles, understanding that with struggle comes strength? What if I could prove the truth of this to you? To do so, I'd like to talk about dragons.

I met one of my first dragons as a young adult during my time with the International Brotherhood of Electrical Workers. I was in my second year of apprenticeship when the foreman escorted me to a muddy field on our construction site. He pointed out a forty-square-foot area about six feet beneath street level, with knee-deep water at the bottom. My job, he explained, was to pump out that water.

Being an energetic, can-do apprentice, I climbed down into the pit with my sump pump and began ridding the hole of water. That water had been soaking into the dirt for days, creating something similar to quicksand. Two hours into the job, my heavy construction boots had sunk so deep that I was stuck in the mud. I spent the next two hours trying to free myself.

After struggling unsuccessfully to free myself, I came

to realize that the only way out would be to create some leverage. I found that leverage in the form of a piece of rebar lodged in the mud. Getting a grip on the rod was not a simple task, however, and required a lot of digging out. But once I got a good handle on it, I was able to extricate myself and slay that muddy dragon.

At one point while I was in the hole, I began to panic. I was literally stuck. There was no one to hear my cries for help. There was no one looking for me. And there seemed to be nothing that I could possibly do to get out. But in spite of that dread, I was able to gather my wits and think rationally, finding a solution to the problem.

I sometimes wonder if that experience was a standard indoctrination for apprentices or perhaps a hazing ritual. I don't know either way, although that type of activity strikes me as being rather cruel. In any event, I faced a dragon in that hole and emerged having slain it.

As in all walks of life, problems constantly arise in the arena of technology. To deal with them, one must suit up in armor and carry an arsenal of weapons to tackle the obstacle at hand. The troubleshooting tech professional is a knight entering the dragon's lair.

And lest you enter unprepared, there is a method to dragon

slaying that must be observed. First, one must delve fully in and welcome the challenge. Second, one must be armed to the gills and ready to combat any eventuality. Finally, one must remain true to the cause and commit to overcoming any hurdle along the way.

While working in Atlanta at MCI Operations Center, my mettle was tested by a dragon I'll call the CTSS 4K, a beast if ever there was one. This analog computer system was used to connect interstate and international calls. It was the workhorse of the original competitive long-distance carriers but was nearing the end of its useful life and was ready to be phased out, coincidentally, about the same time I had become a specialist on it. Because it was handling a workload far beyond the parameters for which it was designed, it required a great deal of my attention.

As the specialist on this technology, I was responsible for the maintenance and administration of the system. Each week, I would run diagnostics on the entire system. And each week, it would be experiencing a matrix failure because the internal wiring was failing. Although the system was still running, it was a significant concern of the company. Furthermore, no one had any idea how to fix it. This would be my dragon.

I was confident that I could figure out what was going

wrong with the system. Having accepted this challenge, I set about arming myself with knowledge, spending countless hours after work researching the matter.

I discovered that the diagnostic was identifying a problem, but after careful inspection, I found that it was reporting it incorrectly. There was, to be sure, the temptation to give up at this point, knowing full well that the 4K system would soon be put out to pasture, replaced by the modern DEX 400. This was a challenge, however, and one ought not shrink from a challenge.

So I began poring through system diagrams, diagnostic routines, related hardware configurations, and cabling specifications. Everything seemed to be in order. Then it dawned on me. The problem with the system may actually be something physical. With a little creative thinking and a lot of perseverance, I ultimately fixed the matrix failure by concentrating on the physics. So when MCI introduced the long-anticipated DEX 400 system, they assigned me to manage it because of the competency I had displayed on the CTSS 4K. My efforts, rather than being vain problem-solving exercises, had yielded tangible results for my career.

The new system demanded, of course, overcoming a new set of obstacles. The move from analog to digital required transitioning from dial-in access numbers to direct-dial long-distance phone calls. That meant installing fraud protection measures and creating equal-access development.

The equal-access aspect played a pivotal role in my future career success, as it was a crucial transition point for telephone companies. To make a long-distance call, you used to dial an access number to get a dial tone. With the new technology, all that was required was dialing 1 followed by the long-distance number.

After mastering the new DEX 400, I became an expert at switching systems. I was one of the few specialists in Atlanta who could diagnose what was happening in a single circuit—from the radio to the internal mechanisms of the switch. Anyone who knows the intricacies of telecom will understand just how difficult that is.

I knew not only the terminal and all of its related components but the computer switching systems as well. As a result of my expertise with the CTSS *and* the DEX switching systems, I was able to demonstrate my propensity for complex hardware, software, and problem-resolution knowledge related to these devices. Having worked extensively with the corporate engineering group as a field system specialist, when corporate decided to expand the laboratory resources in Washington, DC, I got the call.

I was promoted several levels beyond my title at the time to the position of level-two engineer in the switching systems corporate engineering laboratory. Note that there is a direct connection between my promotion into the corporate laboratory and my due diligence with the outdated CTSS 4K system that others had dismissed as obsolete.

Proving your value is essential to your success in any professional endeavor. Regardless of whether or not you work in technology, management is constantly attempting to verify that their employees are worth the price they are being paid.

I've studied martial arts for many years, and one of the first lessons I learned is that you are not facing off against an opponent but rather, against yourself. Mastering martial arts is about mastering oneself. The same principle is true in the professional world. Like any martial arts, regular exercises in self-improvement generally result in success.

A caveat is in order at this point. I've stressed the value of learning, but let's be clear, while gaining knowledge is vital, beware that the acquisition of knowledge is not the end but the beginning. Knowledge without accompanying action is practically useless. Forgetting this important distinction puts you in danger of becoming a professional student. Don't let that happen.

Some people hold multiple degrees but fail to take any action with that wealth of knowledge and float through life unaware of the reasons they've failed to succeed. Often, they may be scared to act, so they just continue to gather more information and store it away. So they end up being permanent students, fail to land job prospects, and can find themselves in worse financial positions than when they started school.

Respect the power of information, but be aware of its limits. Putting your knowledge into action is what actually increases opportunities.

On the other hand, there are some people who become too comfortable with the amount of knowledge and training they have. This is certainly true in the world of technology, but it's universally true as well. These people may be experts in their given field, but if they never seek to grow, they'll miss opportunities without even knowing it.

KEY LESSONS FROM CHAPTER 3

- ARM YOURSELF WITH KNOWLEDGE.

- TAKE ACTION WITH THAT KNOWLEDGE.

- STICK TO YOUR GOALS AND
  LET NOTHING STOP YOU.

- PROVE YOUR VALUE TO THE RIGHT PEOPLE.

- EMBRACE THE OPPORTUNITIES THAT ARISE.

- SLAY YOUR DRAGONS; CONQUER
  EACH CHALLENGE AS IT COMES.

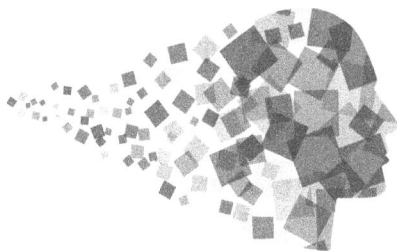

CHAPTER 4

PREPARE FOR THE NEXT CHANGE NOW

CHANGE IS an inevitable part of life and an ever-increasing part of our careers. Embracing and leaning into that change is part of being proactive and the first step to taking control over how change will impact your future.

With the constantly shifting nature of the workforce and technology, the skilled professional looks for parts of these endless shifts to embrace. If an employer asks the team to adapt to a new technology, those who are able to step up and learn that new system will excel much quicker than those who see it as a frustration. The more enthusiastic you are about the coming change, the better chance you have of making it work to your benefit.

A key early step in the process of adapting to change is to find something within the new structure that gives you inspiration. Once you find that thing, hold on to it, and let it become something exceptional to you. Do not just become a master of that thing in general but rather, seek to understand the new elements at play and find the areas with which you feel most comfortable. As opportunities arise within the new space, align yourself with the areas you can approach with ease. Harness your knowledge with the intention of making yourself notable to your superiors. Effectively, you take on the role of change agent by identifying the people, processes, and projects that need to be concisely managed in order to make the transitions as efficient as possible.

The fact is that change can bring with it tremendous challenges, and one must be prepared to accept the trials ahead. In all likelihood, you will see some type of acquisition and merger during your professional career. It's even more likely that you'll experience corporate reorganization. Not all of these company shifts are created equal, however, and they must each be dealt with according to their particular quirks.

Regardless of the various oddities each situation might present, there are some principles that remain universal. Over the course of my career, I have seen several company restructurings. As a result of those experiences, I developed a set of skills to handle them competently.

My recommendation is that if you see a massive change on the horizon, learn as much as you can about the impending situation and use that knowledge to your benefit. For instance, if the company you work for is acquiring another company, you might be fearful that downsizing will put you or your colleagues out of a job. Rather than wasting time being anxious and worried, leverage the opportunity of the merger to acquire a new and valuable skill.

Imagine you're an accountant who has just found out that your company will be absorbed by another one. Use this valuable knowledge to find out everything that you can about the company behind the takeover. During this information-gathering stage, you might discover that the new company has a need for a new IT or human resources department. Although this may not be your direct area of expertise, welcome this moment to expand your value and grow.

Even if you have developed a hard-earned reputation for being an exceptional accountant, when you see the writing on the wall, jump at the opportunity to take some classes in human resources. Go further still and study up on auditing to increase your potential significance to your company. Make yourself too valuable an asset for your current organization to allow a rival company to hire away.

During the process of absorption, you might still get laid off or your entire department might not be needed anymore. Even if you're ultimately unable to convince your employer of your worth, your future job prospects will remain bright because you took the initiative to become more vital to the marketplace as a whole. The amount of jobs and career paths that you can now pursue are much greater.

Additionally, the fact that you have demonstrated an ability to foresee and react to imminent change, along with the experience and credibility you've established in your career as an accountant, will make you a more attractive job prospect in the overall employment market. Worst-case scenario, your company keeps you on in your current position, and you have a hedge against future layoffs and have fashioned yourself into a more well-rounded accountant than the others in your department with whom you will be competing for promotions and raises.

Change is terrifying for most people, and although the advice I have presented thus far may seem logical, most people do not heed it, opting to remain stagnant. German philosopher Friedrich Nietzsche believed that people walk around half-asleep until something wakes them, but he also said, "Once you are awake, you shall remain awake eternally." I take this to mean that most people are stuck in a fixed routine from which they never escape. However, some do. And rewards exist for the people who awaken.

Before circumstances force you to wake up, fight your innate complacent nature, and view every transformation as a chance to lean in and squeeze it dry like a sponge. Adjust your mindset to mold uncertainty into a plan of action, sharpen your skills, be proficient in multiple disciplines, and do all of these things before outside occurrences force it upon you.

In order to fully illustrate my point, I will explain how preparing for transition has impacted my career in one particular instance I was in in Washington, DC, working for MCI Corporate Engineering. As I explained, I was assigned to be the expert on the outdated CTSS 4K. I was fully aware that this system was about to find a new home on a retirement farm upstate, but I also knew the crucial function it still served to MCI, and I knew that I was the only one capable of fixing it in the company at the time when the problem exceeded regular maintenance efforts.

Even though it was flattering to have developers coming to me with the CTSS 4K system's problems, I started to resist the constant state of being at their beck and call every time problems cropped up with the outdated device. By this time, I knew that there was a shift in technology happening, and I had to focus all of my energies into learning the new revenue-producing system. In other words, I was embracing the new, rather than clinging to the old.

While everyone continued to focus on the old system, my manager brought a new device to me and told me to just figure it out, as there was no training budget. This device—a VAX/VMS computer system—was being used in the field at the time and managed primarily by the vendor, but none of the IT managers knew anything about it. Working on the challenging new VAX system gave me the freedom and incentive to avoid the antiquated 4K machine and to start spending more time adapting to MCI's evolution.

One day, a billing transfer was happening at the company when something malfunctioned. It just so happened that the system they were using was the same one that I had been learning: VAX. I was called in to repair the computer because it seemed no one else in the company had any idea how to get the unit back online. I was successful in this effort, and afterward, I went back to my regular duties.

During that time, I decided to create a test bed that looked exactly like the infrastructure for these units. I did so out of a sense of curiosity. After the company found out about my test bed, they put me in charge of all the integration testing for the new computer system, which invariably became the core device for virtually all related operational support systems at the time.

The way that I positioned myself at MCI was orchestrated perfectly. Although some things did, in fact, happen by chance—the computer system malfunction, for instance—the truth is that if I had not been studying and working on my own, I would never have been the expert on the new system in such a short amount of time. I created a test bed for something that was not in my job description, and I did so because I saw the value that it would have to my employer, as the systems made a massive amount of revenue in the field.

It was there at MCI where I really learned to welcome the shift toward new technology, situating myself as an expert even as everything in the industry was rapidly changing. Before long, MCI was flying me out to fix problems at other locations such as Dallas and Chicago. Eventually, I transferred to the national support team and moved out of the lab entirely. I was named senior national support engineer and put in charge of vendor negotiations, implementation, and technical support of the new systems.

If I had let fear of change overcome my emotions during the time, I might have stalled in my career or even been let go during one of many organizational transitions. Instead, I leaned into the change and bent it to my will. In an effort to make myself indispensable to my employer, I made sure to keep my focus on the productive value of everything I did.

When I decided to focus on the VAX system, I did so for a reason. I knew that these systems were revenue generators, so the better I understood them, the more value I possessed. I decided to learn them inside and out. By having the foresight to learn something completely, I was creating opportunity for the future.

I know change can be a scary thing. You may be in a position in which you are accustomed to the status quo, have done well in your current position, and don't know the implications of what's coming your way. However, if you look at each change as an opportunity for growth despite a difficult transition, you may have a chance to dominate in the aftermath. See the change as bringing an onslaught of new opportunities to conquer.

Career transition can be terrifying when you have worked hard to become comfortable in your element. Shifting your mindset from the blindness of fear to the bird's-eye view of readiness will have a profound impact on your career. Remember that things can never improve without some type of evolution or sometimes revolution. But if your mindset is open to the possibilities involved in transition, you are able to act rather than just *react*.

These lessons, of course, extend far beyond the realm of technology, even though that is where my expertise lies. Every industry experiences seismic shifts in the landscape and is constantly evolving. Every employee is faced with the choice of whether to lean in or do the easy thing and stay put. But if your mindset is focused on the acquisition of knowledge as its own reward, you'll begin to understand things on a deeper level, which will then transform obstacles into opportunities and get you through the rough patches. By phasing in to the details, you get to focus on what matters and block out the noise.

It is not enough, though, to simply possess a knowledge-driven mindset. You must be aware of your surroundings and be on constant lookout for the next big thing in your industry. You simply can't rely on your employer to prepare you. Your employer is only concerned with your job duties being fulfilled each day, not *your* future. That onus is yours alone. In today's employment world, you are effectively required to be the chief executive officer of your own career aspirations.

You might be a programmer, for example, working primarily with an outdated software language that keeps antiquated systems functioning. You could easily continue to work with this outdated albeit important software language, only accepting related work for as long as it exists. But you, like that computer language, are slowly becoming obsolete. If, on the other hand, you subscribe to the mindset that I'm advocating, you would be engaged in learning languages that are relevant to the times. By doing so, you would increase your skill set and hence, your value as a programmer.

Ultimately, if you can learn and master one programming language, you have the capacity to learn another. Just like if you're an English speaker who has learned to speak Spanish, then Italian is not going to be terribly difficult to add to your arsenal of language skills. And because you have this valuable capacity to learn languages—any kind of language—do not waste it by not using it. That principle applies to any important skill you possess. If you have it, use it.

So, as stated earlier, lean into any change that arises, and mold it to your will. While you do so, seek knowledge and the acquisition of new skills. Dominate the change in all that you do.

KEY LESSONS FROM CHAPTER 4

- PREPARE FOR CHANGE BEFORE IT
  HAPPENS BY BEING AWARE.

- LEAN INTO CHANGE.

- MOLD IT TO YOUR WILL.

- DOMINATE THE CHANGE.

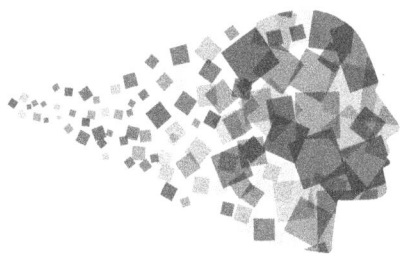

CHAPTER 5

EMBRACE THE STRUGGLE

PICTURE A SIX-MONTH-OLD BABY trying to hold herself up. She falls again and again, yet still vainly keeps on trying to sit upright. Rather than give up at the first sign of struggle, she pushes through. At last, she sits up, giggles, and continues about her development. Afterward, she will never go through that same struggle with the act, having now possessed the knowledge and the ability to sit. That newfound skill is hers wherever she may go.

From infancy, our bodies and minds adapt to struggle. At first, everything is a struggle: sitting, standing, walking, talking. At every level of our development, we struggle toward a higher purpose. Sometimes that higher purpose is as simple as sitting up. As we grow older, that purpose also grows in complexity as we struggle to get along with people, study in school, and excel in our careers.

When I first started weightlifting, I could barely bench a hundred pounds. It was thoroughly discouraging. Although I was a martial artist in good health, I just did not have the physical strength required for lifting weights. I could have easily given up, but I chose to embrace the newfound challenge and stuck with my training regimen. Soon, I was putting on more and more weight, and my strength grew exponentially. What seemed impossible at first had become effortless.

By embracing the struggle, I grew stronger—mentally, of course, and in this case, literally. This is what happens at every stage of human development. Some people hear the word *struggle*, and it invokes deep fear. The word has a negative connotation in light of the fact that we tend to seek comfortable existences free of pain and hardship. However, avoiding struggle has the detrimental effect of making one soft at the core. Moments of strife and difficulty should not be encountered with fear but with determination, as an opportunity to grow stronger.

When faced with something that seems demanding, my

mind tells me to run *toward* that situation rather than *away* from it. In my life, those painful times have always made me feel stronger, smarter, and spiritually more powerful. My instincts now guide me toward the uncomfortable instead of away from it.

At one point in my career at MCI, I dealt with a failing network infrastructure. Every week, the entire network would go down. This was a revenue-producing network, so the company was losing money. My employer had brought on developers, vendors, and other engineers to solve the problem; they called themselves the "Red Team." They couldn't figure out a solution.

They called me, a senior engineer, to try to help with the failing computer system network. At first, I would simply come in and listen at meetings, trying to wrap my head around the issue. After listening to their descriptions, I decided to tackle the problem directly by examining the alarm-messaging feedback at the administration terminal. Although I had little to no idea what I was looking for, I sat for hours upon hours just studying the network and trying to find a way to crack the code.

After days of sitting in front of the computer, tenaciously studying every possible solution, I finally stumbled upon a parameter that looked suspect. By modifying the parameter slightly, I solved the entire problem with the failing infrastructure and saved the company a tremendous amount of money. Needless to say, my job with MCI was pretty safe after that.

Throughout life, we're constantly presented with situations that force us outside of our comfort zones. While it is easy to shrink back and avoid these moments, rewards come to those who are willing to lean in at challenging times. Staying put to remain comfortable has never benefited anyone in their career, or their personal lives for that matter.

As a personal example, I was taking my first international trip to Shenzhen, China, via Hong Kong. It was a business trip, and I was provided with a Chinese interpreter who took me around the city and made sure I was able to enjoy things despite my extremely limited grasp of Mandarin. One of the first places he took me was a village where Chinese families would discuss their culture, traditions, and values.

I'd just finished a full day of business meetings and was still dressed in a suit and tie. My formal attire stuck out like a sore thumb. There was a celebration under way, and we sat down to watch the festivities. Out of nowhere, a performer grabbed me from the audience and pulled me into the performance. I had no idea what was going on, but I played along.

Before I knew it, the prettiest woman I had ever seen was standing next to me on stage, a thin veil covering her face. At that moment, I realized I was part of a traditional wedding ceremony: I was the groom.

After the staged ceremony, we all went to a huge amphitheater and watched a performance full of acrobatics in what I assumed to be the wedding reception. The costumes, the lighting, the music, the whole spectacle was so incredible that I was left completely mesmerized by the experience.

Coming home from that initial trip to China was surreal, and I feel I was never quite the same afterward. As a result of getting out of my comfort zone and going into the unknown, I was exposed to an entirely new world that I might never have otherwise had the chance to experience.

Leaning into the uncomfortable times is something you can apply to multiple facets in your career and personal life. When I decided to go with the flow and allow myself to be a part of the traditional Chinese wedding ceremony, I opened myself up to a new way of looking at the world, and it changed me forever. The same can be said of my decision to take on the challenge of fixing the infrastructure at my company. Diving into the unknown despite the discomfort is a key to development.

Professionally, people grow as a result of strife, and those who clasp on and enjoy difficult tasks are those who grow career-wise. Leaning into challenges and phasing into the details are powerful tools of personal development. When I was first assigned to the task force for the failing network, I had very little knowledge of the infrastructure. Ultimately, however, they designated me as the network "guru," and whenever there was a problem, they would come to me. Due to my resilience in a hard time, I turned into an indispensable force for the company and stood out as someone special and crucial to their operations.

Differentiating yourself professionally increases your career options. Doing so demonstrates a level of ability that your peers may not possess. It also shows that you are not afraid of taking on hard tasks, the sort that others shy away from. Most people don't want to work hard due to a fear of failure. But if you're not concerned with failure—that is, if you view failures as lessons to be learned—you will consistently stick out from the crowd.

When businesses seek to promote from within, they look for people with a proven track record as leaders. Think about it, would you rather be led by someone who has overcome difficulties or someone who has just shied away from them? Those who seek arduous tasks are those who will understand how to deal with them when they arise. Influential people are inherently action takers, and your employer will notice when you take action while others sit back. Be a leader, stand out, and never back away from something if it seems hard.

I have had many chances in my career to show my employers that I was not afraid of leaning into the struggle. At MCI, I eventually earned my way to the third-level support organization due to my work on a failing card authorization computer system because I simply took the initiative to create a test bed to fix related problems. As a third-level support engineer, I had national responsibility to fix complex technical problems that couldn't be corrected by the onsite technical staff or the regional second-tier support organization. As a result, I traveled to multiple cities throughout the country to observe system failures at other sites and fix them.

As a result of this new position, I was tasked with identifying, planning, implementing, and supporting a number of other operational support systems that, often based on my assessment and recommendation, utilized the same hardware. In fact, the utilization of this hardware became so proliferate that I became the de facto expert for all of the operational support systems hardware in use at the time.

An example is when the company decided to use the same hardware device for a nine-city network infrastructure. The infrastructure was built to support a state-of-the-art, at least at the time, operator service platform that included automatic response units similar to what you hear today when a computer on the other end of the line tells you to dial a number to route to a specific location. Because one of my primary tasks was to help the company implement this system, I spent time mastering the ins and outs of the applications that were running on the system. I worked closely with the developers to make sure that they understood nuances of the system they were developing for, and I went back to the laboratory to ensure that I was constantly developing my skill set.

The implementation of this new operator service network application was a great success for the company and the engineering organization that I worked for. We were all very proud that we had the system up and running as planned. We were also quite aware that this particular system had very high visibility in the executive management, so I made sure I knew every component well and mastered troubleshooting problems when they occurred.

In other words, I *phased in*.

At one point during this time, I scheduled a well-deserved vacation. While on holiday, the network began to fail. Everyone tried with no luck to figure out what was wrong. Vendors, software developers, and even executive management tried to solve the problem. They were losing money every minute that the system was down. Finally, my phone rang.

I was in a movie theater when I received a panicked call from my director who explained everything that had happened. I responded that I'd seen that sort of thing before and felt confident I could fix it.

When I told them what to do, one of the software developers took the director aside to say that my idea didn't make sense and wouldn't work. My plan, however, could be implemented in five minutes whereas theirs was a two-hour ordeal. So the director decided it couldn't hurt to try mine.

In less than a minute, the network was back up and running. The company immediately stopped hemorrhaging money. The fact that I solved the problem instantly and while on vacation helped to cement my importance to the company. It all started with my deciding that I would phase in to a deep understanding of the systems that I was responsible for.

I urge you, dear reader, to cultivate this type of mentality. The best experiences in the world of technology only happen once you venture into the unknown. Each journey into the unknown is a door to novel experiences, revelations, and deeper understandings. The unknown has the power to unleash previously hidden talents that you may not even know you possess. And when you delve in, anticipate success rather than failure.

Leverage your abilities in the pursuit of increasing your company's revenue stream regardless of where you are in your career. Look for areas that directly impact customers and that have a direct impact on revenues, then grow and excel in those areas. Again, don't shy away from challenging projects. If you allow yourself to shine, you set yourself apart from your peers and create potential recognition by upper management.

Use the challenges that arise to enhance your career by gathering information and understanding everything that you can about the problem you face. If you're working on a particular device application or software process, acquire the documentation that goes with it, and study it on your own time. The self-studying that you do might not be useful for your current employer, but it may be useful to the industry as a whole.

Cloud computing, for example, is full of unrealized potential even now. And despite its direct impact on nearly every facet of the technology space, expertise in the field is still relatively limited. If your company had adopted it and you were ahead of the curve, you would be impacting your future prospects and enhancing your role as IT specialist. Always look for the next big thing, and if you decide it's of interest to you, make it your mission to own the space.

Now, if you want to figure out what's about to happen next, you have to be in the know. So participate in online forums in your field, join webinars, take online courses, and constantly develop and invest in yourself. I would often pay out of pocket for courses outside my day-to-day requirements because I wanted to know more about a particular subject. There's such a wealth of information available online today that there is no excuse to not consistently develop as an IT professional or a professional in any field.

When you put yourself out there, you'll find that new opportunities present themselves all the time. Just like the baby who struggles to sit up, be actively looking for new ways to struggle to reach your next stage of development.

Difficult problems arise all the time in a technology career, and when they do, there is a specific tiered approach to solving them.

First, understand what the problem is and how is it manifesting itself. For example, you might have a customer who can't access the Internet. That's the problem. But how does it manifest itself? Are the lights off on the router? Is it that nothing happens when he clicks on the Internet Explorer and so on? So you see that it is not enough to just understand *what* is happening. Take the proper steps to understand *why* it's happening. Get to the actual root of the issue.

Second, once you understand the problem, start small and look for simple items first and move in concentric circles toward the more complex solutions. Perhaps the customer is not inputting her password correctly, and that is why she can't get on. That's a simple and easy fix that can be done in seconds. Why would you not try that before a much more complicated and time-intensive troubleshooting procedure? Start with the easy, and move toward the difficult.

When faced with a difficult problem, lean into it. Seek out the dragons that others are frightened of. Highly complex multipage calculation-driven Excel spreadsheets, for instance, can be daunting. Many people only use the tool in a limited and cursory fashion. If not absolutely necessary for one's job, chances are that they'll avoid tackling the intimidating challenge of learning all about the software's capabilities. But if you want your project manager to see that you are tracking things with precise detail, Excel might be a good place to start.

Start small and learn a couple of basic functions that will show your manager that you are keeping track of everything. Eventually, you will continue to get more and more sophisticated with the program, and before you know it, you will have established yourself as an expert with the software, and it will be appreciated by your superiors. If the boss has larger tasks that require someone proficient in Excel, you will be the go-to person for the job.

In mastering Excel, you would have done what no one else felt like doing. Remember that the best experiences in the world of technology and elsewhere happen only when you venture into the unknown. The unknown opens the door for new experiences, revelations, and deeper understanding. Use the unknown to unleash previously hidden talents that you may possess. Take the initiative to expand your wheelhouse. As a result, you will become a go-to person, expanding your career opportunities within and often outside of your current organization.

KEY LESSONS FROM CHAPTER 5

- VENTURE INTO THE UNKNOWN.

- DIFFERENTIATE YOURSELF.

- GATHER INFORMATION.

- UNDERSTAND THE PROBLEM AT HAND.

- COMPLETELY IMMERSE YOURSELF
  IN YOUR FIELD.

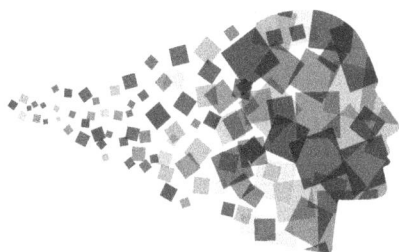

CHAPTER 6

GROW FROM ADVERSITY

LIFE IS consistently throwing challenges our way. Our job is to learn to grow from these trying times. Difficulties present themselves in our careers. We are defined by how we respond. That is the focal point of this chapter. I will explain how to grow from adversity and describe how I was able to rise to the challenge and become a better person in the process.

My first engineering position at MCI was based in downtown Washington, DC. I prefer living in the middle of the action, so being there was absolutely perfect for me. But because change happens fast in technology, I had to be open to the idea of relocating to a less ideal place.

The company moved the laboratory I worked in to Reston, Virginia, which for me was in the middle of nowhere, forcing me to wake up early and commute seventy miles round trip every day. I didn't complain about the adverse situation but simply took a deep breath and continued to do what was asked of me.

One day, MCI announced that the entire Virginia operation would be closing and that employees would have a choice of three new locales that we could relocate to: Dallas, Denver, or Cedar Rapids. None of the choices were particularly appealing, and it took me a while to make up my mind. I didn't have a family to consult with, so I asked my friends for advice. Because I was single, the decision was strictly based on what I wanted to do. While trying to decide where I would move, if at all, a friend mine asked a key question that ultimately pushed me over the edge: "Why not?" After much deliberation, I chose Dallas and never looked back.

I had previously spent quite a bit of time visiting Dallas over the years and was rather fond of the city's nightlife, so when the choices were Dallas, Cedar Rapids, or Denver, well, let's just say Dallas was a shoo-in.

People are often their own worst enemies when it comes to change. We resist what may ultimately be good for us. My company presented an opportunity and was willing to support whatever decision I chose. Getting beyond my resistance to relocate was an inflection point in my life. In the end, I had to overcome my internal struggle, go into the unknown, and move to a completely different location in order to grow in my profession.

Although I had no idea whether the move would result in any career advancement, living in Dallas became absolutely crucial to my growth. Once there, I became the primary engineer for the third-level support group overall, and because I was so well versed in the entire suite of operational platforms, I was promoted to top-level senior engineer reporting to the department director.

Initially, I liked Dallas mainly because I no longer had a seventy-mile commute each day. Now I was about a ten-minute drive from work, making life much less stressful. Although I took logic and a social life into consideration in making the choice to move to Texas, it soon became clear that my emotional state was also improved in direct correlation to the change.

My martial arts experience presents a perfect analogy for this situation. It was something that I fell into later in life, but it has become a major part of who I am. While I was living in Hyattsville, Maryland, I frequented a cafeteria near work that had a martial arts studio. One day, I decided to give it a shot and joined the studio as a white belt beginner.

I was really excited my first day of class and approached the exercise with a great deal of enthusiasm. Well, it turned out to be too much enthusiasm because that very first day of class, I pulled a hamstring while stretching. When I heard a pop, I knew I was in trouble. Pulling my hamstring was one of the most painful experiences of my life, and it happened on the first class that I took. It would have been easy to quit at this point, but I had made up my mind that I was going to earn a black belt, so I worked through the pain and kept going.

Three times a week I hobbled into class to do what I could despite my pain and limited range of motion. There were times when the pain was so great that all I wanted to do was wrap my leg up and watch television. But my mindset had an intention that required my action, so I refused to stop. In actuality, I can't say that I kept giving myself pep talks to stay motivated. Instead, I was operating on autopilot, letting my mindset manage the flow without questioning until my hamstring healed and the pain subsided.

Over time, I became one of the best students at the studio and progressed through the ranks at a rapid pace. This was due completely to my mindset of becoming the best student that I could be. Nothing was going to stop me once I made the decision to continue through the pain.

The martial art that I studied was tae kwon do, and the school I attended was quite aggressive. We spent hours in battle, fine-tuning our skills to the point of automatic response. My head instructor seemed to be a natural at getting the best out of his students, and I really appreciated his level of expertise.

To succeed as a martial artist and earn a black belt, one must have a great deal of perseverance. When I started my practice, I was already in my late twenties and deeply invested in my career. I worked every single day, and then I went to the dojo for three hours every night in order to hone my craft. I was constantly tested with various physical and mental challenges. If you do not have mental strength, you will not succeed in martial arts, which requires consistent practice, correctly executing the different forms, and overcoming your tendency to take the easy way out.

Throughout the process, there were times when I just didn't have it, where my spirit on any given day was low, or my energy depleted after a hard day at work. There were definitely times when it was a tremendous struggle just to show up. But my mindset, no matter what, would not let me quit and carried me through times when training was especially difficult. After all, it is diligence that makes the difference between people who actually attain the rank of black belt and those who just dream about it.

And what was the biggest battle I faced as a martial artist? It wasn't my competitor in the statewide competitions I participated in. Nor was it the overly aggressive black belt who would periodically take pride displaying his superior skills at our expense. It wasn't even the out-of-control young guy who felt it necessary to throw and kick as hard as he could to prove himself. No, the essence of training in martial arts is to vanquish a far more powerful opponent: yourself.

And your best weapon against this opponent is your mindset, for it is your mindset that musters the will to stretch a little further, punch a little harder, kick a little higher, and move a little faster. It is your mindset that refuses to allow you to give in to fatigue, both physically and mentally. It is your mindset that moves you to overcome the stress of competition, to work past the boredom of repetition, to show up when your whole body says, "Just give me a break."

It is your mindset that feeds the intention to overcome the obstacles and builds the will to embrace the struggles. This is the same mindset that allowed me to take on the difficult task in technology, to risk failure when attempting to resolve network failures that others had given up on, to do battle with stubborn electrons, face down deceptive software, and force hardware to comply with my will.

So remember this when faced with adversity, weigh out all the options, and evaluate a variety of perspectives. Always make logical rather than emotional decisions and realize that the biggest opponent to your growth is your inner self.

Think of every problem as a mile that must be walked. At first, you might not feel like walking a mile, but if you take the first step, it starts to seem achievable. Then you walk a block. Soon afterward, half a mile, and before you know it, what once seemed arduous is now highly manageable. Think of every problem in terms of a mile, and just take it one step at a time, just like a new martial arts student earns one rank at a time.

KEY LESSONS FROM CHAPTER 6

- GET OUT OF YOUR COMFORT ZONE.

- LEAN INTO ADVERSITY.

- REALIZE THAT YOUR BIGGEST
  OPPONENT IS YOUR INNER SELF.

- OVERCOME YOUR OWN LIMITATIONS.

- MAKE LOGICAL DECISIONS RATHER
  THAN EMOTIONAL DECISIONS.

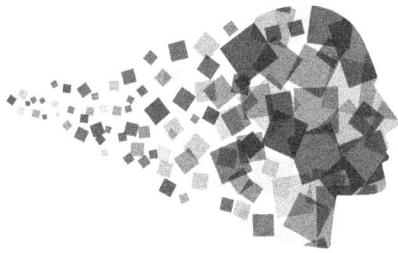

CHAPTER 7

MANAGE YOUR MINDSET

EVERY SUCCESSFUL PERSON, at one point or another, takes some time to establish a mindset. For me, my mindset was always to seek new information. I cemented this into my brain at an early age, so whenever an obstacle would present itself, my goal would be to use the knowledge that I had acquired to overcome that hurdle. If I did not have the understanding, I would go out and find it.

After I decided that the acquisition of new information was paramount to my success, I used that mindset to establish my intentions, which from the get-go were always to overcome whatever life threw at me. Nothing would ever be too much to handle if I could master the requisite skills to accomplish a particular feat.

Once I had established an intent to overcome obstacles, I translated that intent into a clearly identifiable action. Without action, neither the deepest-ingrained mindset nor the noblest intent holds any value. Attaining the next level of success, whether in one's career or personal life, requires action based on an accumulated amount of knowledge necessary for that particular advancement.

Those actions will present us with a variety of paths to follow. Although we have one particular outcome in mind, it's critical to remain open to multiple lanes of possibility. In my journey thus far, the path has not always been clear, but I remained and continue to remain open to varying routes along the way. If there's a secret to success, this is at the core of it.

I encourage you to consider who it is you want to be and where you want your life to go. Those answers will guide you when the path is murky or when the going is rough. A precise vision of who and where you want to be is the basis of a plan of action that will take you ever forward even as others around you meander aimlessly in circles.

As for your mindset, it need not be the same as mine.

Maybe the quest for knowledge does not resonate as soundly with you; maybe you are driven by a desire to serve humanity or build relationships or some other noble ideal. Whatever your mindset, be clear in it so that you can establish your intentions, which you will later act upon. Act swiftly, without doubt or hesitation, when decisions inevitably present themselves.

Once you discover what it is that makes you tick, you will want to steer your journey in that direction, which requires finding a purpose and acting upon it. For me, that meant reading, studying, taking courses, listening to mentors, and immersing myself in the knowledge that I sought. In so doing, I've become the person I've always wanted to be.

To become the person that you want to be and to get to the place in life that you want to occupy, you have to start with the fundamentals, and that means establishing a mindset and developing a purpose. Once you do that, you will have substantially whittled down your available range of options in any given situation. That's not a bad thing; in fact, it's a very good thing. Without a purpose in life, you have an infinite amount of choices that present themselves to you at every turn.

With so many possibilities and no clear goal in sight, how can you know which decision is best? On the other hand, if you have a desired aim, the right action will usually be obvious, eliminating for you any confusion about what to do next.

If you know that you want to be an expert in your field, being up-to-date on the state of your industry will reduce ten thousand possible actions at any given time to a handful. If mastering your profession is your life's desire, the choice between taking advanced-level courses in that field or joining a kickball league is a no-brainer. Your purpose will dictate your course of action.

When you have alignment between action and purpose, you are dwelling in a harmonious state of being. It's like having a script in life rather than just improvising it scene by scene. That's no way to make a movie, and it's certainly no way to live one's life.

Mindset is absolutely crucial for success, as it establishes a subconscious internal intention. I have yet to see a strong-willed mind accept defeat.

While living in Texas, I decided to give back to the community by joining a state-sponsored mentoring organization called the Texas Youth Commission. The focus at the time was primarily on inner-city youth, particularly teenage boys. I'd often sit with them and ask about their lives, the central question being, "What do you want to be when you grow up?" Based on their answer, I could tell immediately who was going to succeed and who, unless they made a change, was going to consistently struggle through life.

Many of the kids had no clue what they wanted to do with their lives and were clearly just going through the motions, following the examples of others who often had no clarity for their own direction. Many inner-city kids tend to have incredibly poor role models and generally establish a low bar for their aspirations in life way before they reach adulthood. Worst of all, they do so without ever realizing that it is often the consequences of their choices that dictate subsequent outcomes.

Some kids I met, however, were different. They understood that they could do whatever they wanted with their lives. They had dreams and aspirations. Some even had plans about how to achieve them. Unless they went down the wrong path, I knew that they would succeed in something based simply on their way of thinking. They knew that they wanted to make a better future, and they understood that it all started with the right attitude.

A mentality is, for the most part, created during the teenage years. If surrounded by excellent role models, some people may develop a clear outlook even earlier in life. I knew that if I wanted to reach out to people while there was still hope, it was important that I reach them as teenagers while their minds were still malleable and before they lost the ability to dream big.

Once you know who you are, that knowledge will be reflected in everything you do. Renowned former University of California, Los Angeles, basketball coach John Wooden used to begin every season by teaching his team how to put on socks. Socks! We're talking about elite college athletes like Kareem Abdul Jabbar and Bill Walton. Coach Wooden ensured that there were no wrinkles, folds, or creases; the socks were tight and smooth. This, of course, is essential in preventing blisters. A preventable blister will slow down a player, which means that it will slow down a team. Coach Wooden understood that there was a right way to go about things and that if you followed that path, your chances of success would be greatly increased.

Regarding the socks, Coach Wooden would explain to his players that the lesson contained everything that they would need to know in their lives. The idea being that how you do the simplest of things—things that other people take for granted—is emblematic of how you do *everything*. If players are meticulous about how they put on socks, you better believe they are meticulous in executing plays on the court. That mindset, Wooden understood, manifests itself in everything you do.

The attention to detail that Coach Wooden exercised was a foundational element to establishing a mindset of top-tier performance. Once this is ingrained, you will find that you perform at high levels in virtually everything you do. Subconsciously, you will be putting yourself on autopilot, achieving goals without even realizing exactly what you are doing at that moment. This method is a bulwark against pessimism and negativity and will enervate you as you strive toward your goal.

While I was working for MCI, I learned to connect devices, routers, and bridges through the network infrastructure. I learned the language that these instruments use to communicate. I understood not only the devices doing the communicating but also the devices in between that allowed for that communication. I mastered the network circuitry and protocol language that made their communication possible.

The acquisition of knowledge was always paramount during this entire process of mastery. Once I gained expertise with each device, I would begin to focus on how the computers talked to one another. I understood the hardware, and I also understood the application and operating systems for the individual components of the network. My constant and tenacious pursuit of knowledge led me to master several different functionalities at MCI and advance in my profession.

This knowledge came in handy when I was assigned to participate in a NASDAQ project that involved the buying and selling of stocks via application code. This particular application code was using protocol language to initiate orders, and the network was having issues communicating.

I taught myself the language that the network was using to communicate and ultimately solved the problems the company was having. That success brought another project: Advanced Intelligent Network (AIN). This assignment was similar to the prior one: it was hampered by something, and nobody had been able to figure out what that something was.

Because my mindset was such that I was not going to be deterred, and my purpose was to be a technology guru, my course of action lay itself out before me like a red carpet. I might not have known at the time what the solution to the problem was, but I did know how to figure it out—one step at a time. And once again, that method proved itself successful in accomplishing a herculean task.

I read the manuals, created test plans, talked to others who were experts in various aspects of the overall project, and totally immersed myself in the theory of AIN. The more I learned about the protocol, the more my desire grew to know about the protocol. For a while, I was totally consumed by my thirst for details and data. In the end, I solved the problems, implemented the system, and delivered the customer requirements. Although there were significant challenges along the way, my intention was clear, and perseverance won the day. Ultimately, it was my never-ending reach for knowledge, put into action, that allowed me to accomplish the goals that laid before me.

Even as I describe the work I've done with technology, there is another factor that I would be remiss if I did not address: the human element. It can't be overlooked. Early in my career, I was so analytical that I dismissed interaction with other people as ineffective. I was very brash at times, and if someone did not move as quickly as I wanted, I would get frustrated and do that person's job myself. Learning to be a team player did not come naturally to me, and I strained a lot of professional relationships unnecessarily.

Neglecting the human element is a grave mistake in one's career. In the realm of technology, it can be easy to forget that we are all on the same team and are supposed to be working together. After all, we are simply a village, albeit on a grand scale, and we must communicate with one another and work in unison. It's imperative to speak the language of your peers, direct managers, and executive management if you wish to advance in any endeavor. I've been in job cultures where my peers required a relaxed, cooperative language, often talking sports or family before talking shop. Managers, however, were often under stress and required deep dives into the subject matter, spending very little time with small talk. Executives, on the other hand, were not interested in deep-dive conversations or presentations. They always looked quickly for the bottom line, and any conversation outside of that was focused on problem solving to ensure sufficient attention to revenue impacts. Knowing the language on these levels is key to communicating effectively.

KEY LESSONS FROM CHAPTER 7

- ESTABLISH YOUR MINDSET.

- ALLOW THAT MINDSET TO BUILD INTENTIONS.

- TAKE ACTIONS IN LINE WITH YOUR INTENTIONS.

- UNDERSTAND THE LANGUAGES AROUND YOU.

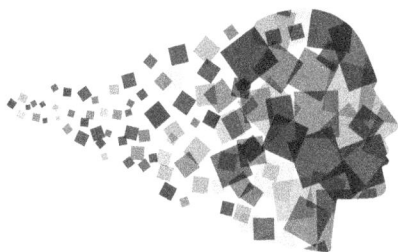

CHAPTER 8

EXPECT TO SUCCEED

ATTITUDE IS ALTITUDE, as they say; a positive attitude is a formula for climbing high. The key to maintaining a positive attitude is by managing expectations. Pessimism can kill even the best of intentions because it often triggers an emotional response that drives away focus. A major goal of any kind requires focus, and a negative attitude zaps energy from your purpose, wasting it on unhelpful, diverging thoughts.

Moreover, attitude has a residual effect in that it builds upon itself to create momentum in one direction or the other. Positivity breeds positivity, while negativity breeds negativity.

The expectation of success is often the *reason* for that success. As far as expectations are concerned, you essentially have three choices: no expectations—which might not even be an actual state of mind but rather, a state of denial—or you either expect to succeed or to fail. If you have the ability to influence your expectations, and I'm here to tell you that you absolutely do, then why would you sabotage any positive development by setting yourself up to fail?

I was once asked to take on the role of senior business development manager in the international marketing department, which certainly wasn't on my radar given the career path I'd been on. However, because I took the initiative to work on a project outside of my purview, I opened up a whole new field for myself. It was certainly not the path of least resistance. I could have opted to stay where I felt safe and comfortable, but because I took on the role with the expectation of succeeding, I was able to do so without dwelling on the possibility of failure, which is a direct route to failure.

This idea of focus is similar to walking or driving a car. You will naturally veer in the direction you are looking. Try it for yourself sometime. (Try it on a walk, rather than behind the wheel of a car.)

Unless someone really is out to get you—and maybe not even then—know that you are your own worst enemy. There is something inside each and every one of us that will second-guess our talent and ability and that is likely to get bogged down along the way to wherever we are going. You can't get there if you're tripping over your own feet. To ensure that you are moving fluidly in the right direction, visualize yourself being successful. That vision will not in itself create success, but it will certainly pave the way for it to follow.

This visualization technique is something athletes do to achieve success in performing an action. Basketball players often close their eyes and picture themselves hitting nothing but net right before shooting a free throw. Golfers will visualize the path of the ball as it rolls into the hole right before a putt. By seeing success, we can focus our gaze in that direction and veer closer toward it.

You will experience many small victories on your life journey. Rather than immediately moving on to the next endeavor, always take a moment to breathe in the sweet smell of success. This exercise is not a mere pat on the back; it has real psychological effects.

First, it serves to help you identify with victory. This identification is powerful, as that association provides momentum. If you think you're a winner, you'll tend to do the things that winners do. If you feel you're a loser, you'll tend to see failure as your natural state of repose.

Second, that positive feeling you have when you take a big whiff of your own accomplishment creates a habit-forming desire to re-create. Whether you celebrate that success by lighting up a good cigar, enjoying a glass of fine Scotch, or by treating yourself to a full-body massage—whatever it is that you do, even if it's just smiling—it releases a flood of dopamine in your brain, making you feel good all over.

By taking that moment to savor your small victory, you are actually developing a reward-based behavior pattern that your mind will seek to emulate again and again to elicit more dopamine, basically making you a success junkie.

The project I mentioned that led to my being asked to take on the role of senior business development manager required that I take time to understand the process of business development, which is very different from planning, building, and supporting networks. So I did have to roll up my sleeves and approach the position from a different perspective than what I had been accustomed to. And as I became more proficient at business development efforts, I took time out to recognize my growth and reward myself with a little self-satisfaction, which was all it took to propel through the entire process, creating the impetus necessary to complete the mission at hand. In other words, I celebrated the small victories.

Even if your small victory is merely gaining knowledge of how something works—and do not underestimate the value of understanding the working of things—pause and reflect in order to drive yourself forward.

Every little success you experience along the way will feed your emotional bank account and give you the confidence necessary to persevere. While failure after failure will drain your emotions, small wins will replenish them. As you deal with obstacles, of which there will be many, take the time to make deposits into your emotional bank account. You will gain poise and become more assured of yourself in the process. When the next obstacle presents itself, you will be more than ready to face it.

Think about the act of dreaming. When you are dreaming, everything seems real. Unless it's a lucid dream, you are not conscious that you are in a dream state. Your senses are still operative here—you can smell fragrances, see colors, taste flavors, touch objects, hear music, and generally do everything that you can while you're awake. If the mind can do that while you are asleep, why couldn't it translate that information to an awakened state? The power of the mind is yours to create intentions that will allow you to get through even the most difficult tasks. If you can visualize yourself completing a massive project, you simply have to wire that into your brain.

This concept is a lot like muscle memory. There are actions that are required to perfect a tennis serve. The first time you try, you'll probably get the timing wrong or you'll put the ball into the net. You'll also be very conscious of each micromovement, the position of your body, the location of the ball, or other thoughts. These conscious thoughts slow you down. When you master the art of the serve, you will do it as unconsciously as breathing. Your body's muscle memory will do it automatically, allowing you to focus on higher aspirations such as strategy or gamesmanship.

Believing in oneself is critical to achievement. If you do not truly believe in yourself, your mind will put you on a different course. If you remove all doubts, on the other hand, anything is possible.

Modern communication technology is a prime example of our ability to overcome obstacles. The way that we communicate now is exponentially more advanced than even a hundred years ago. The technological advancement and developments during the last century would not have been possible if our innovators had resorted to negative thinking and disbelief. Perhaps instead of an electronic medium, we would still be telegraphing communications.

The expectation to succeed can be a catalyst for success, as Michael Jordan proved during his National Basketball Association career. Jordan famously said, "I've missed more than nine thousand shots in my career; I've lost almost three hundred games; twenty-six times, I've been trusted to take the game-winning shot and missed. I've failed over and over and over again in my life. And that is why I succeed."

Jordan's entire philosophy and state of mind are clear from that one quote. Despite those setbacks, he never allowed the doubts to influence his mindset, which was that he expected to make the shot and win the game. And because of that positive mindset, he won six championships and established himself as the greatest basketball player of his era and probably any era.

There was a period at MCI that I had been assigned to several separate projects. I was juggling the aforementioned NASDAQ project, a network systems project, and a fiber restoration application. Naturally, there was a temptation to feel overwhelmed by the magnitude of the workload, but because I had a clear intent in mind and an expectation of success, I was able to focus on and succeed in each task, earning a promotion to senior engineering manager.

The skill set required of a senior engineering manager is quite a different arsenal than what I had developed to that point in my career. It demanded managerial and interpersonal communication abilities that I had not yet cultivated. I put my doubt and insecurity aside and began to listen and learn, intent on becoming a good manager.

Once I established that intention, I rapidly began progressing in my capacity as a manager. Soon, I was given added responsibilities and tasked with acting as a liaison between engineering and the global wholesale department, a role that required that I supervise communications between the two.

In this capacity, I was asked to devise a plan to grow business development in emerging markets. One of my first opportunities came with a dialogue with a major North African telecommunications company that was having real challenges with its aging communications infrastructure. Because of the volatility of this particular area of the world, there were a number of executive-level managers who were adamant that we would never be successful in acquiring any type of business contract from the related incumbent. Although their opinions were highly respected by senior management, they left the door open for me to see if I would be able to generate any business despite the difficulty expressed.

For a while, I reflected upon the problem, initially deferring the bulk of the conversation to the naysayers while I looked for opportunities to move the project forward. I was not convinced, as they were, that we could not win a contract in this region of the world. To the contrary, I had a suspicion that there was a pathway to success in this endeavor and probably subconsciously looked for ways to overcome obstacles that were presented.

It wasn't long before such an avenue presented itself through a network of resources that gave me the opportunity to interface directly with key decision-makers within the potential customer's organization. You see, in this particular case, it was paramount that the customer contacts we were engaging for business development discussions had the authority to make decisions for the company. As a result of significant investigations, I was able to identify the proper pathway to the decision-maker and invariably won a lucrative contract with this company. Through determination and for the most part, sheer force of will, I was able to overcome naysayers and other difficulties I'd faced.

Success in that endeavor bred further success, as I was

flown to countries all over the world to help evaluate global technology projects and grow business development. Somehow, I had risen from a workbench in a lab to high-powered meetings with corporate executives. I knew from the start that there was value in learning all that I possibly could and expecting to succeed, but I never imagined that it would result in my traveling the world to use interpersonal skills.

Once again, as I continue to reiterate within the pages of this book, my mindset, intentions, and action resulted in new pathways toward success. First, I mastered a hardware device to become the best troubleshooter in the company for that device. Mastery of this initial device resulted in more responsibility and growth within the corporate engineering department.

As a result of being in corporate engineering, my scope of responsibility increased significantly, effectively providing more opportunities to take on the difficult tasks that others avoided. Assuming and resolving difficult problems put me in line for continuous promotions in the engineering discipline, which led to my becoming a senior engineering manager, which in turn opened the door to being a technical liaison between engineering and international sales, resulting in my role as a business development manager with a global footprint.

My point in sharing with you this illustration from my own life is to confirm for you the value of cultivating positive expectations. It has tangible real-world effects that I have experienced firsthand. You may not know from the start exactly what those effects will be, but you don't need to. Just know that they are probably beyond the limits of your imagination.

Instead of asking "Can I do it?," begin to start asking, "*How* can I do it?" The two questions are 180 degrees apart, as they begin with different assumptions. The former is born from a place of doubt while the latter begs the question of "Can I?" and skips right past it, asking the next logical inquiry, "What method will I use to accomplish it?" Just by rephrasing the question, you will alter the way in which your brain is wired, and as a consequence, you will become more effective in your endeavors.

KEY LESSONS FROM CHAPTER 8

- QUASH YOUR DOUBTS.

- PAY ATTENTION TO YOUR
  MINDSET AT ALL TIMES.

- CELEBRATE SMALL VICTORIES.

- DO NOT LET NEGATIVITY TAKE
  CONTROL; STAY POSITIVE.

- ALWAYS EXPECT TO SUCCEED.

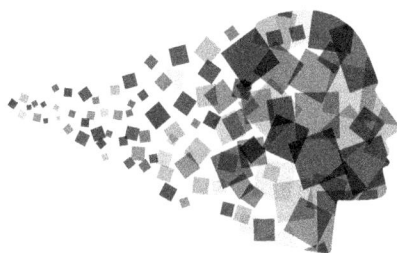

CHAPTER 9

PHASE IN: FOCUS ON WHAT MATTERS

TO BE HIGHLY SUCCESSFUL in any profession, you must possess the skill of focus. If your intentions change because of your mood, the weather, or some other factor, you're going to have problems achieving the goals you set in life. To avoid this, you must phase in and focus on what matters.

Begin by ensuring that when you start a project you are crystal clear on what is being asked of you. Pay close attention to the details surrounding your assignment and adjust your decisions and actions accordingly. If you hone in on the intricacies of the duties, you will begin to discover that every task has a specific set of nuances. The distinctions that make a given project unique are the details on which it is critical to phase in.

At MCI's Global Wholesale Group (GWG), I was the person who would be sent in to evaluate the technical requirements of a particular job. Technological requirements, as you might imagine, are incredibly distinct, and I was tasked with convincing executives to accept the necessities of the work that we were doing. The core of the job, however, was understanding the customer's needs. To do my job well, I had to ignore other unrelated issues and focus on what was actually needed by the client.

Human beings, it turns out, are the most crucial component of any project. You have to understand people on some level to garner long-term success in your field. Although I worked in IT, I continually sought to foster my so-called people skills.

During my business development travels, I was often sent to countries with completely different cultures. It was not always clear who the real decision-makers in a room were, and that was significant information to me in my role. I paid close attention in one country, then another, as I began to phase in, developing a keen eye for posture and other body language, as well as when and how people spoke. It proved to be a critical focal point.

I learned that in some cultures, there is a reluctance to give bad news. There is a desire to spin everything in a positive way, not because they are lying so much as that it's simply considered good etiquette or because the person you are dealing with is not the actual decision-maker and isn't allowed to respond in a brutally honest manner. If you're sharpening your interpersonal skills, your gut will start to kick in. You will begin to intuit when someone is painting a rosier picture than the reality suggests.

For example, there was a point when I was in London, meeting with a potential customer who represented a large construction organization in the Middle East. This customer was seeking consulting services in support of their pending bid to build an entirely new city that would be considered a jewel for increased commerce and technology for the region. The attendees of the meeting were all senior-level executives, and I had a pivotal role understanding the customer's requirements.

The meeting was going well, and I was quite excited to get started as this would be a windfall for our business development efforts, yet something seemed a bit off, and my cautionary intuition began to kick in. So I began to ask some basic questions regarding the overall aspirations of the customer. After a few leading questions, I began to feel that maybe things weren't as they seemed, so I proposed we adjourn the meeting, and I would work on a proof-of-concept proposal for the customer to review.

My thinking was that if the potential customer was truly in position to win this bid, the proof-of-concept review would give them the opportunity to identify clearly their support requirements from a consulting entity such as ourselves. If they were unable to give clear direction upon review, we were probably just being used as a name-recognition organization to further their agenda, without the downstream benefit of actually being hired to perform the work. The action I put forth exposed the latter, and we saved ourselves tens of thousands of dollars chasing a phantom.

You might wonder what clued me into the questionable sincerity of the potential customer—"posture." Their posture, despite their words, screamed a level of insincerity that was clearly evident to me. During the initial meeting, whenever we delved into the complexity of the project from a management perspective, it was quickly dismissed by the principle negotiator of the company we were interfacing with. If the question of allocated budget was broached, their body language said that this was something they hadn't considered, although the words they used were "Don't worry about that. We have the budget." It just didn't feel right to me. I should mention that no one else on my team actually saw this but were very appreciative that I did.

Reading posture or body language is a learned behavior, although we all have that ability as humans to do so instinctively, mostly at a surface level. To be able to read deeply, so to speak, requires a bit more focus and experience, something that I picked up over the years as a product of my intention to be good at human interaction.

One of my most important tasks was to figure out who could make decisions within an organization and woo that person to my way of thinking. That would be simple if it was just a matter of titles. It's tempting to think that a senior vice-president would be able to pull the trigger on a deal, but in fact, I've encountered senior vice-presidents with little or no actual decision-making power. Knowing who pulls the strings requires a laser-like ability to focus on matters of importance such as sphere of influence and resource control.

Human communication is highly complex and heavily layered and often resembles a game of poker. In poker, people often provide subtle clues about what they are thinking but not saying. After a while, in fact, if you become skilled enough in reading body language, you stop listening to the words that are actually being said and focus your attention on what is *not* being said, what messages are being communicated bodily.

Human communication is important knowledge regardless of the profession you're in, and I strongly recommend that anyone reading this book begin a study of it now. Chances are at some point, you will find yourself in a meeting with someone who is smiling and nodding as you talk about an idea, but the person's body language is telling a different story. The more you know about what makes people tick, the more success you'll have in all areas of your career and personal life.

Phasing in to a *goal* is much different than phasing in to a *project*, however. Goals have the tendency to become overbearing. This, of course, is why people often drop their goals when they become difficult. New Year's resolutions are the classic example. People start off with good intentions, but when things get too hard, they drop their goals completely. Gyms are bustling in January, but by April or May, they're right back down to their regular attendance levels.

Failing at goals is demoralizing, so people often stop goal setting entirely. Goals tend to be long-term, marathon-like propositions. That can be intimidating, as we all know. However, when you phase in, you are less likely to give up when times get rough. Simply take it one step at a time, and complete your goal incrementally. If you want to get a master in business administration, for instance, stay the course the entire way. Find out which classes you need, meet with an adviser, and slowly reach your goal.

Phasing in is what makes goals possible to achieve. The idea is to see the big picture while taking actionable steps along the way. You'll find more success by seeking out teachers, coaches, tutors, and personal trainers than by going it alone. In addition to the accountability factor, experts provide the steps you need to reach your goal.

If you want to shed a hundred pounds, it will probably seem impossible at first. But when you work with a trainer—one workout at a time, one day at a time, one meal at a time—that large, faraway goal becomes incrementally closer. Rather than focusing on the entire hundred pounds, change your focus to the very next pound, and you will see progress, which will keep you from falling into despair.

Phasing in applies not only to your personal goals but is just as relevant in a corporate setting. In that context, it's important to try to understand three critical elements: the company's language, its culture, and its management's expectations.

Every organization has its own internal vocabulary and terms of art, which you should look to master from the outset. There are always acronyms, and you need to know what they stand for. Learn the language quickly and begin using it.

Understand whether the culture is such that you wear a suit and tie or jeans and a button-down shirt. Are you expected to participate in team-building activities, such as a co-ed softball team or ping-pong during afternoon breaks, or even attend happy hours? Be aware of the vibe that the company is trying to create, and fit in because it really does matter.

Additionally, management may put many different unofficial pressures on employees that they will expect you to figure out. There is always a hierarchy in any company, and knowing who can and who can't ask requirements of you is a necessity. In some company structures, you will have access to senior-level management, while at others, approaching your boss's boss is seen as an end around and is severely frowned upon.

Absorbing this unwritten code of conduct requires presence of mind. If you are present in every situation, you will notice small details that others overlook. You will be aware of imperceptible changes in the air and know that something is amiss without having to be told. That knowledge is often the little difference between being prepared for change or being a victim of it.

If you're the type who comes to work wearing headphones, zoning out and isolating yourself from your colleagues, don't be surprised if you're kept out of the loop on important matters coming down the pike. Whatever your chosen profession, communicating with people is necessary to your success. Even if your job entails sitting at a cubicle and working in solitude, and even if you're introverted by nature, it's still important to interact with your coworkers. You just never know how those relationships will benefit you in the future, but they inevitably do seem to open new doors in my experience.

Your cubicle mate today just might be your boss tomorrow. The person you pass in the hall each morning might be called upon to vouch for you if your company downsizes and you both end up at a new company. Never miss the chance to build relationships because they are fundamental to your success.

This idea of relationship building also applies outside of the office as golden opportunities are all around. Plant seeds in your community, and they will grow. Your world will expand with new possibilities. The hard part will be choosing which avenues to travel down and which to avoid. However, if you're clear about your intentions, you will have the discernment to know which paths will showcase your talents allowing you to excel and which are not worthy of your time.

As I pointed out before, the most important projects are those that directly affect a company's bottom line. When you're doing your homework on your company, determine what it is that brings in revenue, and look for ways to increase it. Upper management will take notice of your efforts, and promotions are only a matter of time.

During my traveling days with GWG, the company assigned me to a group of technical experts in remote locations such as Bahrain, United Arab Emirates, and Jordan, among others. On one particular trip to Bahrain while fulfilling my role as liaison between the engineering department and global sales, I attended a business development meeting that was focused on reviewing a request for proposal for a network infrastructure bid.

The first day of the meeting, I applied my usual strategy of listening and remaining quiet in order to learn as much as I could from the conversation and from what was being communicated nonverbally.

The first thing I learned was that I knew absolutely nothing about the proposal that was being discussed at the table. That's a major problem. I went to the hotel that night and completely phased in on the two-hundred-page document. While studying the document, I marked every section that had issues and made extensive notes about it as well.

The next day, I presented everyone with the issues that I had flagged in my studying the paperwork. The room was very impressed with my assessment. In response, the company designated me as the person charged with the first read of all related proposals and technical documents. By phasing in on the two-hundred-page document and keeping my mouth shut until I had something useful to add, I was, ironically enough, recognized as an expert.

There was another instance that bears mentioning. This time, I was in another country in the Middle East, and there was an ongoing project that required modification to continue. Despite many attempts by our executive team to reach agreement with the local incumbent, efforts to get contract modification were stalled.

After doing a great deal of research, I discovered that the primary reason we were unable to get the necessary contract modification done was because up to that point, we were negotiating with low-ranking people who lacked the authority to sign on the dotted line. Having discovered this, I took on the task of identifying the proper authority, engaging that authority, and getting the contract modified according to our requirements. Identifying the decision-maker enabled us to get the deal done—a task that previously seemed impossible.

A final example regarding the power of phasing in will further serve to illustrate my point. I was in Istanbul to discuss a project that would greatly enhance that region's banking network infrastructure. After reading and evaluating the customer request for proposal, it was clear to me that the task articulated in the document would require a high level of technical functionality and therefore, cost to implement.

Taking on a project of this magnitude required immense resources and was not to be entered into lightly. I wanted to make sure that the customer was aware of the estimated cost of a project of this nature, given their expectations of functionality for the network infrastructure.

Internally, however, there were parties who simply wanted to put a process in place that would superficially provide some level of functionality, while not really providing the full functionality that the customer was asking for. It was clear to me that if we provided the scaled-down version being proposed by others, we might win the contract but would put ourselves in a position of having a very dissatisfied customer at the end of the day.

I phased in completely from the customer perspective and pushed back on providing the scaled-down version. Instead, we provided the actual cost projections for a fully functional network that met all of the customer's requirements and made it clear that we would not implement an infrastructure that failed to meet the specifications being requested. At this point, we encouraged the customer to reconsider their related budget allocations and stepped away from the project.

Rather than being merely anecdotal, these examples should also serve as proof of the power of phasing in. The efforts I made, which others might fairly classify as extraneous, were necessary for me if I was going to advance my career in the direction I wanted to go. As a result of following my own internal compass, focusing on customer service as a prime directive and taking the time to fully analyze the project requirements, my deep dive into a number of initiatives were successful. To wit, I was promoted to be a direct report of the GWG senior vice-president.

A singular focus on a specific problem will allow you to achieve anything you want in your professional life. Find the one identifiable core issue on which you want to concentrate, then seek to understand that issue in its entirety. Maintain a presence of mind as you do, and rely on your communication skills—verbal and nonverbal alike—to pinpoint the location of your focus.

Similar to warfare, the idea is to use reconnaissance to discover weak links and then focus your concentration there. Phasing in is the equivalent of this strategy.

KEY LESSONS FROM CHAPTER 9

- PAY CLOSE ATTENTION TO DETAIL.

- DO NOT GET SIDETRACKED BY UNIMPORTANT PROJECTS.

- MAINTAIN A PRESENCE OF MIND.

- BUILD YOUR COMMUNICATION SENSES.

- FOCUS ALL YOUR ENERGY ON THE MOST IMPORTANT TASKS.

- PHASE IN COMPLETELY TO ACHIEVE SUCCESS.

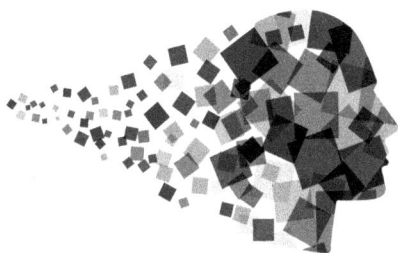

CHAPTER 10

MAINTAIN EMOTIONAL CONTROL

A MOOD, by definition, is a temporary state of emotional being. If your moods dictate your actions, you are not in control of your destiny. And success requires that you shape your destiny, that your actions align with your purpose. While it is important to acknowledge your feelings, those feelings must not be the driving force behind your behaviors.

During the course of my career, I developed a strategy

of observing and listening before speaking in meetings or discussions. This would make many of my colleagues uncomfortable; they were used to having more boisterous employees sitting in meetings. But rather than cave to their expectations, I stayed with my approach because I knew myself well enough to know that what I was doing worked for me.

Had I been more moody, I might have allowed my emotions to turn sour, filling me and the room with more negative energy. However, my practice of mindfulness created a bubble in which the emotional reactions of others were unable to penetrate and influence me. By keeping my feelings in check while I waited until all the information was in, I established myself as the calm voice of reason amid a chorus of rash emotions.

Learning to manage your emotions takes time and is a lifelong process. Everyone has had the experience of lashing out in a heated moment and ruining a relationship or an experience. If left unchecked, emotional outbursts, which escalate already-difficult situations, will continue to make matters worse in one's life and inevitably lead to regrets. Pausing to take a deep breath, on the other hand, will steady the emotions and pave the way for reason to take the helm once again.

Educating yourself about human psychology will not only enhance your interpersonal communication skills but also your ability to harness your feelings when necessary.

Emotions often run high in a business environment, as different personalities and philosophies collide and interact. Every department within an organization—sales, engineering, customer service, administration, and so on—have their own agendas and are pursuing their own goals, even as they serve the purposes of the company as a whole.

I've personally seen many working relationships ruined because of unchecked emotions. In Atlanta, for instance, I witnessed a coworker become enraged at something a manager said. Instead of shrugging it off, he turned and punched a hole in the wall. At that point, management was forced to make a decision about his future with the company. They let him go.

If he would have paused, taken a deep breath, and just let it go, he would definitely have kept his job and progressed further within the company. Instead, he completely ruined that working relationship and possibly future prospects in the field. Interestingly, he had been slated to lead the implementation of a new network operations center, a job that I ended up getting.

The key to controlling one's emotional state is to compartmentalize it by keeping your eye on the big picture. When I was in North Africa, I worked with a fellow prone to emotional outbursts. I did not let his actions affect me at all, and I stayed true to course, keeping my focus on the mission at hand.

It would have been easy to act out in the manner that he did, but it would not have been productive to my goals in any way. Although I was genuinely upset about the situation on occasion, I put that anger into a different place in my mind, where it would not hurt my career, goals, or character.

The fact is that when we are under pressure, it can become harder to manage our reactionary impulses to outside stimuli. When you're tasked with meeting a sales quota or delivering a presentation to a group of C-suite executives for the purpose of winning their business, patience can wear thin. Yet, these are the moments when you show your true mettle.

To be calm in the storm or to be the force that brings order to chaos is one of the most impressive attributes you can have in life, not just the world of business. It takes practice, though. It also requires that you have a mindset in which this attribute matters to you. I can simply tell you that over my career, this is one attribute that has served me well. I suspect that if you adopt the same, it will serve you well, too.

Every day, we make choices about how to react to situations, yet most people do not consider how their actions impact the people around them. You might be driving down the street when someone suddenly cuts you off and sends you into a rage. In that moment, you have the choice to flip them off or let it go. You could easily retaliate and cut him or her off as well, but this would not do either of you any good.

Not only would you ruin your state of well-being, but you have no idea the effect it might have on the other person. That person whom you flip off might take his or her aggression out on others. Now you have possibly triggered a domino effect in which innocent bystanders become collateral damage as a result of your aggression. Always be mindful of how your actions might affect others, whether immediately present or not.

When you make the decision not to respond in kind, you take away the power of that negative moment. Staying away from these types of conflicts is healing and keeps you on your path. Conversely, engaging with others negatively will deplete your emotional bank account and end up hurting you more than that other person. It might also create a tit-for-tat feud that carries on in perpetuity. If you manage to keep the small things from bothering you, there are benefits to be reaped.

It's easy to stray off course when dealing with stress. When I was working as a technical liaison for international sales, I would often be in meetings in which people would look right through me or worse, turn to the other person in the meeting and speak only to that person, ignoring me. I realized that this was likely some form of bias, but I refused to take it personally.

If I had become personally offended every time something like this happened, I would have lost my focus completely, and they would have essentially won. Remember that reaction of others to you says more about *them* than it does about *you*, and responding in kind only brings you down to their level.

While I was in Jordan on a job, I experienced an event that tested my emotional control. I used to stay at a beautiful Western-style hotel that had a downstairs lounge. Over time, I had become good friends with the bartender, and we would chat it up while the band played in the background. I loved being in that environment and meeting new people, so I was there nearly every night meeting people and enjoying the music.

One evening, I got called into a meeting at the hotel. Usually during this time, I would be in the lounge listening to the band. While we were waiting for the other people in our meeting to arrive, we heard an explosion. Everyone started screaming, and we were rushed out of the room.

A suicide bomber had blown himself up in the lounge, killing members of the band, security guards, and even one of the bartenders. I was completely in shock and distraught over the fact that I could have easily been there that evening.

Despite my team's emotional state, we contacted the customers we were supposed to meet and ended up walking to their hotel that night and moved forward with our agenda the next day. Although I was obviously upset, I did not allow my emotional state to detract from our mission. We met with the customers, made progress on the deal, and moved on. No one would have blamed me if I holed up in my room until it was time to catch a plane back to the States, but I made a choice to control my emotional response and stay focused.

The clients were extremely impressed that I was able to maintain composure and meet with them anyway, although I have to admit that the terrible images that I saw the night before were unnerving. I can still recall the faces of some of the people who were lost that night. When I finally returned home, there were people who now saw me as someone they could count on even when things got rough, and this type of dependability made me one of the survivors within the company.

Again, always keep the big picture in mind. Do not allow emotional stimuli to derail your entire mission. Although you may want to retaliate, there is little value to doing so. If you switch off that response mechanism, that stimulus will completely lose its power.

Keep your key mission in mind at all times. If you're a project manager working with a team and you notice friction between your team members, resist the urge to get involved. Remember that you are the boss; take steps to mitigate the risk. The ability to compartmentalize your emotions should be practiced in all scenarios.

Next time you are driving and someone cuts you off, take a deep breath and practice letting it go. Tell yourself, "He or she must be in a bigger hurry than I am," and just let it pass. As you continue to practice this, you will gain the skill of emotional control.

KEY LESSONS FROM CHAPTER 10

- FOCUS ON YOUR KEY MISSION.

- KEEP THE BIG PICTURE IN MIND.

- NEVER LET EMOTIONS DICTATE ACTIONS.

- PRACTICE CONTROLLING YOUR EMOTIONS.

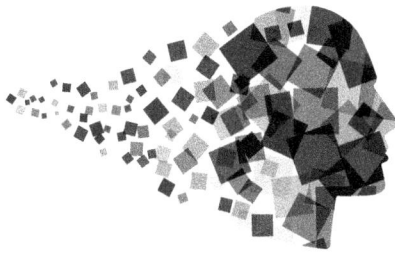

CHAPTER 11

SHOW UP AND COMMUNICATE

THERE WILL BE times in your life when you will want to give up or just don't have the desire to do anything at all. Perhaps you are physically exhausted, stressed, or just feel like staying in bed. These moments are a test for all of us. We could easily give up and stay home, but there would be consequences. People who are able to fight these feelings are able to keep momentum in life and achieve more than others because they have learned the importance of showing up.

Showing up is at least half the battle in anything, maybe more. As Woody Allen puts it, "Ninety percent of life is just showing up."

Maybe you do not feel like exercising, but you show up at the gym and do your workout. Maybe you do not want to go to work, but you go anyway, and you do your job. Maybe you do not feel like attending a family function, but you go anyway, and your family appreciates seeing you. Showing up is vital to the human experience because if we are not present, we miss everything.

When you feel particularly low, take a deep breath, get over your hesitancy, and forge ahead. There are many times I am scheduled to give a speech but do not feel confident about speaking publicly—especially when it involves speaking to high-level executives. It's easy to get a case of nerves. I can feel their eyes on me and endure their scrutiny.

In those moments, do I turn around and drive home? Of course not. I press on, get into motion, and the presentation flows naturally. I establish my mindset to one of action, and I get energized as a result. Rather than thinking of it as a scary presentation, I see the event as merely a friendly dialogue.

Showing up means getting over your negative thoughts, engaging and allowing yourself to live completely in that moment.

It is not enough to simply be present, though. Once you show up, you have to communicate effectively and be prepared to do so on multiple levels. If during the course of a public speech you use my technique of thinking of it as a conversation, you can become more comfortable in it. The experience will not have changed, but you will have.

There are studies that suggest that some people fear public speaking even more than death. The fear comes from the thought of being criticized, embarrassed, or appearing foolish in front of others. When you shift this frame of mind into a focus on communicating your message, you can present to anyone without letting fear overcome you.

Once you do that, you can focus on communicating on multiple levels. Begin by controlling your body language, facial expressions, and gestures to be consistent with your message. If you are giving a sales pitch and your body language communicates that you do not want to be there, your message is not going to be received well.

You also need to be well dressed and enthusiastic; your appearance needs to match your message. Everything you communicate verbally and nonverbally should be aligned.

My career is centered around advising, consulting, and sharing information. In fact, information influences nearly every industry. In order to properly share it, you must first master understanding it, then be able to give advice that is consistent with the overall mission of those with whom you are communicating.

Once you master something, you will often have people coming to you for advice. Many are worried about sharing their knowledge, and they hold on to it in fear of losing something. You must not be afraid to share what you know with others. When you lift other people up, you lift yourself up, and the energy comes back to you tenfold.

When you share freely with others, it creates positive momentum. When you share with others, they will share with you. Although you might be a master in one arena, the person you are coaching may very well be an expert in a field that you would like to pursue. If, for instance, you are a consultant, and someone asks you for information you possess, you could blow him or her off. In doing so, however, you are shutting that person out and essentially ending the relationship.

Instead, share that information with him or her freely, and he or she will grow to value and respect you. That person might not ever become a client but could refer someone to you in the future or provide you with a lead on a potential job or career shift. Become an ambassador of your own brand, business, and professional reputation.

It is also vital to document your accomplishments. I recommend keeping a journal and engaging in self-reflection. As humans, we tend to always think forward and reject the notion of pausing and reflecting on what is happening in the moment. We automatically go through the motions of life without considering what it all means.

Imagine yourself preparing to take a vacation trip. If you're anything like most people, your mind is entirely focused on anticipating the journey ahead. You are thinking about what you are going to do, whether you have packed everything you might need, and your experience of being in that new location. When you finally arrive, all you can think about is going back home and getting back to work. You are not present before or during the experience, constantly living in the future. Thus, you are not maximizing the experience, being too preoccupied elsewhere.

Being present allows you to embrace the moment and experience it fully. If you are present during your vacation, you can go back to that moment over and over and relive it in your mind. You just might want to mentally revisit that tropical beach or wherever the next time life gets too stressful. If you were really there, experiencing it fully, you will be able to draw upon it to get you through the hard times.

The practice of being present directly relates to communication. If you are talking to someone who is not present in the moment, it will be apparent. If you are thinking about other things, you will miss the other person's message and will be unable to respond appropriately.

Practice the art of creative listening by actively engaging, rather than just waiting for a bottom line or planning what you will say next. When you listen creatively, you are completely present in the moment and gain a deeper level of understanding.

The practice of being present goes back to self-reflection. I often reflect back at the end of the day and ask myself a series of questions: *What did I do today? What did I experience? With whom did I experience the day? What things of value did I provide to others? How did I engage with the world? How did I make a difference? What types of conversations did I have? Did someone cut me off in the car? How did I react?*

I will go through my entire day, sometimes in my journal and sometimes in my head. When you self-reflect, you take time to think of how you felt in moments throughout the day. Doing this enables you to see patterns, habits, and behaviors you can correct in the future. You can then make adjustments in order to live a more productive and positive life.

If you are working in the technology field, I highly recommend that you keep a journal. Journaling will allow you to gain a deeper understanding of your discipline and gain insights into problem solving. You might deal with a particular problem one way today, but in a few months, you will have a completely different reaction to the same issue. The process of writing things out is not only therapeutic, but it can also give you a deeper understanding of your strengths and weaknesses.

As I mentioned before, journaling can also be a way to document your accomplishments. Later on, you can look back at all the cool things you did with a certain company. Then, when you are being interviewed for a new position, you can share those rock-star moments with confidence. Management can trust you because you are tried and tested, and you recognize problems when they reappear.

At some positions, I was even required to keep a journal. When I would go on vacation, whoever was in the lab would inevitably be unable to solve a problem and contact me. Due to the process of consistently writing out my mental thought patterns, I was able to fix the issue with ease. The practice of writing out everything allowed me to internalize my methods and be able to convey them to others.

Showing up and communicating has been paramount in my career. When I traveled, I would often be in strange situations in which it would have been easy to act shy and subdue my personality. I would fall into this trap often, as situations are so unfamiliar when traveling to foreign countries. If this happens to you, do not beat yourself up about it. It is a natural instinct to want to protect yourself.

Embrace your shyness in those moments. If you are an introvert, feel good about your introversion and use that to your advantage. Extroverts might be better at speaking to others, but I would argue that introverts tend to listen more closely and often analyze social situations at a deeper level. Look for opportunities in which you can engage on topics that you know, and leverage the skill of asking questions to build relationships. Do not fight your true nature; find a way to make it work for you.

You might find yourself at a conference and end up engaging with someone about football. Perhaps that person knows nothing about the subject but is interested in rugby. There is a common ground that you can find there that can be educational for both parties.

Professionals often become too obsessed and single-minded in their own field to have normal human conversations with others. Doctors, to give but one example, who spend all of their time talking to colleagues about the practice of medicine, might struggle to discuss any topic outside of that area, despite the fact that they are college-educated people and interact with people outside of their own profession as part of their daily routine. With this in mind, look for opportunities to connect and communicate with others on a variety of topics.

You may be asked to give a presentation to an executive team at some point in your career. Do not shy away from the opportunity to share what you know. Just know who your audience is, and speak to their needs. Many times, people give a PowerPoint presentation without thinking about what their audience actually wants to hear. Instead, take the time to learn who your audience is and what information they are seeking from you.

Suppose you've been asked to address a group of board members about a particular technical topic. It is worth pausing to consider what aspect of this actually matters to them. It just might be that their only concern is the revenue-producing component of the technology. If that's the case, you'll want to tailor your entire talk to that one section and give them plenty of time to ask deeper questions related to what they want to know about. In so doing, you will be providing value and not wasting their time.

Strive to show up and communicate effectively. Reject whatever preconceived notions you might have about your personality flaws. Present fluidly and communicate on multiple levels, verbally and nonverbally, aligning your message in every way. Focus on whatever your audience is looking for, and turn your presentation into a conversation. Despite your doubts, take a deep breath and show up—that's the hardest part after all. The momentum of that will usually carry you the rest of the way through.

You are here on earth for a purpose. Whatever your religion or philosophy, acknowledge that you have a mission in this life, and that is why you are here. We all have a mission, and our value lies in that mission. It is critical to bear that in mind.

As an IT and telecom specialist, my mission is to help people share information and communicate over vast distances. When I do that, I am doing my part to help subdue the earth.

Whatever task you take on that serves a collective purpose, be sure to take the time to clearly understand how your role influences the overall outcome. If you can apply this mentality to every discipline in your life, you will find new meaning and purpose. This is the pathway to true leadership.

The thing about leadership is that once you display it, you'll find yourself thrust into this position again and again. It just seems that people naturally detect your leadership abilities and continually put you in this role.

For example, when it was decided that the company wanted to develop a business unit around growing professional services in emerging markets globally, I was tasked with leading the process and increasing our related business development efforts.

KEY LESSONS FROM CHAPTER 11

- SHOW UP.

- HAVE THE CORRECT BODY LANGUAGE.

- DOCUMENT YOUR ACCOMPLISHMENTS.

- LEARN THE PRACTICE OF JOURNALING.

- COMMUNICATE ON MULTIPLE LEVELS.

- BEGIN TO UNDERSTAND YOUR TRUE CALLING.

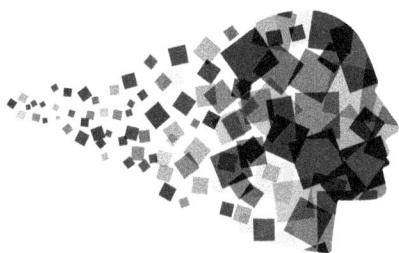

CHAPTER 12

TO WRAP IT UP

MY CENTRAL MESSAGE is "Believe in yourself." Whatever you are doing and whatever industry you are in, believe in yourself unconditionally, passionately, and without apology. You are a unique person. Your presence touches people, and it sometimes touches them for a lifetime.

Many people have believed in me. Their presence in my life has made a huge impact. One of my high school teachers, Mr. Daudy, had absolute belief in the fact that I could conquer electronics. His confidence in me was so matter-of-fact; he helped to reinforce my budding aptitude for technology.

Another influential example was Mr. Crystal, the owner of a grocery store across the field from my house. All of the neighborhood kids would frequent his store to buy candy and soda. He was always jovial, friendly, and loved being around kids.

One day, I was sitting in front of the TV when I heard a loud boom ring out across the field. It was Mr. Crystal's store. Someone had tried to rob him. As he was reaching for his gun, the robber shot him. That was a sad day for many of us. Just thinking about it gets me emotional still. He had such a profound impact on me and my community.

You never know the impact that your life might have on someone. Your contribution to the world matters, whether it's overcoming a technical obstacle, smiling to a stranger, giving a public talk, or helping someone in need. You make a huge impact on the world whether you realize it at the time or not.

Cultivating a strong practice of knowing and loving yourself is critical to development. If you are having problems loving yourself, stop and realize your true purpose in the world. No matter your current station in life, you do have a purpose. It doesn't matter if you're the trash collector who wakes up every day at 3:00 a.m. or the construction worker who builds housing for people; you're making an impact and adding value to the world.

If you have doubts as to your purpose, take a moment to reflect on the value you bring with your unique skill set, personality, and talents. Seek to maximize that value by learning more, serving your community, and making contributions wherever you can. The more self-love you have when you pursue things, the more joy you will find in life and the more that happiness will be spread to others. You will, as a result, bring exponentially more value to your community and to the entire world.

We all have the power to improve our lives, and we can only make things better when we properly care for ourselves. When you come from a place of love, you will seek to improve yourself, working constantly toward that goal. There is nothing you cannot accomplish with love, and you will be an unstoppable force.

Having a mindset centered on the belief in oneself is the basis of success. In youth, that sense is often derived from our parents or other elders. As a young man, I had a strong sense of who I was and knew that I would get out of school, into the professional world and make something of myself.

When others would laugh at my ambitions, it would only reinforce my determination to achieve. Something inside me was alive, and in retrospect, I know it started with a firm concept of my independence. I consistently took steps toward self-sufficiency, as I knew that that was my true goal. Moreover, I felt I deserved the best that this world had to offer and knew without a doubt that I was going to acquire it.

Once I had established my mindset, I set an intention to find the mechanisms to bring about the fruits of my desire. Those mechanisms led me in the direction of technology, which I followed without ever looking back. I mastered my field, learning a multitude of technologies. There is virtually no technology I cannot quickly understand and adapt to. All of that was born from self-love, a mindset, and a clear intention.

I have applied the concept of mindset to every facet of my career. In the field of IT, there are numerous ways in which changing one's thinking will lead to possibilities that were once unimaginable. IT is all about communication. Computer systems, data storage, project management, and application codes are just tools for interaction between elements, with the goal of providing value to a process or a project. So, with the knowledge that technology can be boiled down to communication and interaction, you can adapt your mindset to reflect that.

An IT specialist in application programming ought to think beyond just programming. Consider what it is about programs that matter, that provide value. Consider what the value of programming is to your company. Your purpose may very well reside in that answer.

Your responsibility on an app coding project might be very small, but that doesn't mean it isn't necessary. In which case, the entirety of the project hinges on your work. Therefore, value your role. Take a different view of your contribution—as being significant—so that when you are writing that code, you are doing it with the intent of the mission at hand. Your value tremendously exceeds your responsibility.

If you throw a tiny pebble into a lake, the ripple extends so much farther than might seem warranted by something so small. But that pebble is influencing a group of water molecules, which in turn, influence even more water molecules, and so on and so on. Such is life. Your life, whether professionally or personally, might directly impact only a handful of other people, but those other people will impact still more people, who will, in turn, impact still more people. That is the power of your influence.

Armed with such power, actions are amplified to the benefit or detriment of an exponential number of lives. Common sense suggests that our decisions be sound, and to that end, the input of others becomes all the more necessary, especially when that input comes from a diversity of experiences.

Instinct, or intuition, is another voice that ought to be heeded, as IT professionals tend to rely overwhelmingly on logic and experience. Nevertheless, intuitions are a valuable source of information as well, and we would do well to heed their advice. Intuition has been a guiding force in my career even if I didn't know at the time why I was experiencing it.

We've all experienced intuition at some point in our lives whether we've heeded it or not. When I was sixteen, I went to a party but had a bad feeling about the place when I got there—nothing tangible, mind you, just a negative vibe in the air. I suggested to a friend that we stay by the door. There was a loud slap moments later, and pandemonium erupted. We got out quickly and safely because we were by the door.

Intuition is a sense that requires a lot of practice before it can be trusted but once trusted, is quite reliable. You trust your sense of vision because you have been using it every day of your life, but it wasn't always as reliable as it is today, assuming, of course, that it hasn't been damaged in some way—staring at a computer for long hours perhaps.

Your sense of smell is probably less refined as it isn't quite as necessary for survival. If it's in good shape, you might be able to articulate a few notes on the bouquet of a wine or detect a hint of jasmine from a block away. If you use that sense more, as any wine or flower enthusiast will testify, the sense will grow stronger. So, too, will your intuition.

Part of trusting yourself in your professional life means developing an *entrepreneurial* spirit rather than an *employee* spirit. Employees seek to be told what to do by a boss. Entrepreneurs take risks and seek to consistently find ways do more with what they have; they also look for ways to solve problems rather than blaming others.

Instead of just following the plan that has been laid out, look for ways to develop further outside of that mission. I did this by always going above and beyond what was required. I took courses on my own to master technology, and I sought new knowledge everywhere I could get it. If you think like an entrepreneur, you see that new knowledge always presents more opportunities.

When I wanted to learn the new computer system at MCI, I was told I should continue with the technology in front of me. Rather than blindly follow orders, I decided to learn it anyway. When I was put in the laboratory, I found a way to expand beyond just working on the device I was assigned and turned that device into a test bed for a revenue-generating operational system—not because anyone told me to but because of my independent spirit and the desire to add more value.

Each time that I sought new knowledge without being asked, a new opportunity appeared for me to grow within my profession. Whether you own your own business or are in the corporate world, it is important to think of yourself as a businessperson and treat your job as a business that you are in for yourself.

At one stage in my career, I decided to forge my own path and get certified as a Project Management Professional (PMP). To do this, I needed to pass a difficult test and study on my own time. I never told anyone at work that I was doing this, as it was only for my own personal growth.

One day, the senior vice-president of GWG approached me about program managing a cloud infrastructure build. He had no idea I had already attained the credentials and was ready to manage the entire project. When it came time to program manage this initiative, I was not only ready from an experience perspective, but I was also certified to do so by the governing body of the industry standard: the Project Management Institute.

I took the initiative on my own to advance my credentials, then reaped the benefits in time. If you wait for others' permission before bettering yourself, you will always be trailing someone else. If you grab life and lean into challenges, however, when opportunities arise, you will be ready to handle them before anyone else.

One final anecdote is relevant here, as it changed my entire perspective on life. My grandmother gave me an 1883 silver dollar when I was eighteen. When I turned twenty, I fell on some hard times. I began selling virtually everything I owned just to stay afloat. I even sold that silver dollar. I sold it for $7.

Thinking back on it as I write, I want to cry. It's not about the money. I miss my grandmother so much that I would give anything to hold on to something that she gave me.

At the time she gave it to me, I failed to see its true value. I wasn't present enough in that moment. I wasn't present in the moment either when I sold it. I didn't realize its significance. Because of that, I lost something I could not replace.

Be present always. Take time to make smart decisions, and realize that the true value of something—whether it's an old coin your grandmother gave you or your role in a project—is not always evident at the time or from your current perspective.

KEY LESSONS FROM CHAPTER 12

- ALWAYS BELIEVE IN YOURSELF.

- PRACTICE SELF-LOVE.

- KNOW YOUR VALUE.

- BE PRESENT IN ALL THAT YOU DO.

PARTING THOUGHTS

YOUR MISSION on this planet is much larger than you may think, and by doing your part to help others in whatever way you can, you expand that mission exponentially. Don't take your value and contributions to the collective lightly. Discover what your mission is, show up, and communicate it effectively to others. Be the star that shines brightly, providing light in the darkness of night. And most importantly, be sure to *Phase In* to your purpose. The world needs you to.

ABOUT THE AUTHOR

DAVID RICH is a certified business process management professional. He blends a technical background in IT with telecom expertise and strategic business acumen in order to increase profits, develop accounts, and drive operational performance.

David has an MBA from Keller Graduate School of Management, and applies it daily to help plan highly technical projects with multi-million dollar budgets. Over the years he has proven his skill in defining a vision, mapping strategy, and developing domestic and global markets. His international acumen has helped him establish and evolve key accounts in the Middle East, while setting up complex network integrations and cloud infrastructure initiatives.

Delivering a comprehensive understanding of the market, technology, processes, and human capital of the IT/Telecom Industry is what David is most passionate about. He generates best practices with a creative approach and recognizes the value of far-reaching networks. David welcomes brainstorming and collaboration in several areas:

- STRATEGIC PLANNING

- NETWORK IMPLEMENTATIONS

- PROGRAM / PROJECT MANAGEMENT

- PRODUCT MANAGEMENT

- CLOUD SERVICES

- CARRIER ETHERNET

- BUSINESS PROCESS MANAGEMENT

David lives in northern Virginia.